John

Leave it to Naasu

HOW TO TAKE CHARGE AND GO FOR WHAT YOU WANT

NAASU GENEVIEVE FOFANAH

It's so lovely to see
you again!

Best wishes

Naasu

Nfofanah.

R3THINK PRESS

First published in Great Britain in 2020
by Rethink Press (www.rethinkpress.com)

Contents

Introduction

My daughter and Oprah Winfrey

Twenty years ago, on a sunny afternoon in Gettysburg, Pennsylvania, my daughter JJ arrived home from nursery with her father. I got up to give her a motherly hug and wait for my usual update about her day. I told her that I would help with her homework. To my horror, my assertive and extremely independent four-year-old replied: 'Ooooh mummy, you can't read or write. All you do is cook, clean and watch Oprah Winprey.' (She couldn't pronounce Oprah's last name.) I felt so demoralised and inadequate. My circumstances had clearly influenced my little girl's perception about my ability to support her academically. Indeed, I was in a dark place in my marriage, but this indictment was a catalyst to take charge of my life and act on my aspirations, regardless of the consequences.

My daughter was right; I was guilty of exactly what she had described. When she returned from school, I would have meticulously cooked, cleaned and be relaxing on the sofa watching Oprah. I was a stay-at-home mother by choice, mutually agreed with my husband when I became pregnant. But just as golf and Tiger Woods provided relaxation for her father, Oprah was my solace, inspiration and strength during a difficult marriage. I would listen to her and to 'Dr Phil'; many of the beautiful, sad stories resonated with me.

In 1999 I wrote to Oprah about a backpack project. JJ and I were frequent flyers with Virgin Atlantic since she had been born in 1995. In those days the airline gave children a red backpack filled with lots of fun things to entertain them, while adults received strong, plastic backpacks. Many of the empty backpacks were left behind on the plane. Sometimes, I would gather them up to send them to Sierra Leone for school children. Being a huge fan, I decided to write to Oprah about my backpack project. To my surprise, I got a response not only acknowledging my email, but showing an interest in my project. She said she had been thinking about doing something in Africa and thought my idea was good. I couldn't believe that Oprah had actually replied to me. Off I went to share the good news with my friend Gina; we became overrun in Oprah mania. Unfortunately, my marriage became untenable and I separated from my husband, returning to London with my daughter to start a new life. I'm not sure whether Oprah tried to contact me again, but I was extremely pleased when Gina told me that Oprah had indeed made it to South Africa and was doing amazing work with girls. Her Leadership Academy for Girls is a wonderful initiative for the empowerment of girls.[1]

The core me

My cousin Zainab summarises me as an enigma because people who assume they know me truly don't. This is understandable because although I appear outwardly accessible, inside I am hard to reach. Therefore, when I make myself available to people, they assume they know me. But I know exactly what 'my core' is. She is the strategic chairwoman of my being who draws me back when I try to deviate from my mission. My mission is to be faithful to myself. Firstly, I am a good person who is happy with herself whatever the circumstances. Secondly, I believe in humanity and doing positive things to support others. Thirdly, I use challenges as opportunities to build resilience and make strides in achieving what I want and, in exceptional cases, what I need. I do not hold grudges; I speak my mind honestly and take full responsibility for the consequences. The core me is resilient, thoughtful and fearless. I am a spiritual and

---

1   https://owlag.co.za/

generous person. I am very principled, and that sometimes gets me into trouble. The core me is complex, but
I am humble, respectful and easy to get along with.

However, I have some fundamental principles that I
won't compromise. Betrayal and dishonesty are death
sentences to a trusting relationship. I find it difficult to
recycle trust in anyone who has intentionally hurt me;
I prefer to transfer my energy to more fulfilling matters. This helps me to counteract any psychological
impact and makes it difficult for me to hold grudges.
I examine what happened and accept my share of
responsibility in every situation in order to maintain
my emotional wellbeing. I am a committed and decisive woman who believes in living on equal terms in
a just world.

My journey

I am enormously proud of the woman I have become,
despite the challenges I have gracefully endured. I
stayed true to my core self. Every chapter of my life,
regardless of the experiences, has made me a better
person. From the five-year-old girl to the fifty-year-
old woman, I have impacted people's lives by standing up against injustice, both for myself and others.

Growing up I was not expected to become the woman
I am today. My prospects, based on my family's socio-
economic status, destined me to complete secondary

school and get married to a 'decent man', not neces-
sarily a rich man. Higher education was out of reach
and travelling overseas an impossibility; they didn't
even occur to me. But I knew what I wanted, and I was
going to get it despite the barriers that I constantly
faced. I was not going to become a casualty of the system, although everything pointed in that direction.

My mother said that when I was five I told her that
I would let her fly in an aeroplane. I must have been
fascinated by the planes that landed near my primary school, bringing dignitaries to town. Although
it wasn't clear how I was going to keep this promise, I
was committed to it; in 1997 I organised for my mother
to visit me in London – naturally, by plane.

Although higher education seemed impossible, I was
determined to get there, even though I didn't have the
cognitive awareness of exactly how. I just knew that
a lack of education would be the only real obstacle in
achieving my ambitions. I made this a lifetime crusade and worked relentlessly towards it. I now have
a Bachelor of Science (Hons) in Psychology from the
University of Westminster, a Master of Arts in Education, Gender and International Development from the
Institute of Education and University College London
(UCL), and a Joint Executive Master of Public Administration from New York University (NYU) and UCL.

Being married is an important achievement in my
cultural context; many negative assumptions are

attached to single women. Although my marriage ended within five years, it did mean that I fulfilled that socio-cultural obligation. More importantly, it gave me the opportunity to become a mother, something that is one of my greatest achievements. Motherhood has taught me what pure love entails, and I work hard to create a better environment for my daughter than the one I grew up in.

Travel seemed another impossible childhood dream. Although my father went to the United Kingdom to study as a Signal Communications Specialist while in the Army, there wasn't so much as a glimmer of hope of me going abroad. Today, I have travelled the world and it has broadened my mind. It has also allowed me to experience different cultures and traditions which has increased my understanding of the world.

I've experienced several dark episodes in my life. These include a suicide attempt when I was six months pregnant and almost becoming a stroke victim at just twenty-nine. These harrowing episodes made me re-evaluate my life: what made me happy, what my passions were, and how I could meaningfully contribute to humanity. I suffered extreme loneliness and had to fight both physical and emotional battles. My crusade to stand up for vulnerable people, especially women and girls, stems from my lived experiences of injustice and abuse. Through my struggles I have managed to find solace and carve a path to a lifelong commitment to women and girl's empowerment.

Although I went to university as a mature thirty-one-year-old woman, my professional progress has been impressive, including serving as Adviser to the Executive Representative of the United Nations Secretary-General and as Special Gender Adviser to the President of Sierra Leone. My professional trajectory has been rewarding and given me a global perspective on life. I have also had the privilege to work in national politics and gain an insider's understanding of how my country is governed.

Returning home after several years abroad to support post-war reconstruction of Sierra Leone was one of the best decisions I ever made. Ten years down the line, I have contributed immensely to our national development agendas both as a public servant and as a private citizen. From entrepreneurship to political leadership, I have positively influenced the discourse on women's and girls' empowerment across the spectrum. I have challenged the status quo and fearlessly led campaigns. These include violence against women and girls – particularly sexual violence – reproductive health rights, women's political leadership, and issues around cultural rites of passage.

Looking at where I am now, I see a woman of great courage and resilience who gets things done. I took up challenges that seemed impossible and made them happen. My experiences have kept me grounded, allowing me to prioritise and deliver on my aspirations. Despite the hard work, I know there are still challenges that require personal sacrifice and further learning to realise my ambitions, but I feel equipped to face them as they arise.

One of my dreams is to see an Africa with more women presidents and political party leaders. Our continent will never achieve her highest potential without inclusive political governance at the Executive level. We must have more women presidents within the African Union to leverage the abundant possibilities from the continent. We must harness the untapped potential of our women as a key natural resource for development. We women must step forward and open spaces that are closed to us, using our numbers to influence meaningful change. Women must disrupt the political status quo as a priority to Africa's transformation.

I decided to enter full-time politics as a commitment to the global and regional call to have more female political leaders. I joined the Sierra Leone Unity Party and was appointed Deputy Chairperson/Leader. The party intends to field as many women candidates as possible, including candidates for President and Vice President, in the 2023 general elections. This progressive initiative will see the Unity Party joining parties in different countries to lead the charge for inclusive governance in Africa. Although I am well aware of the structural and systemic impediments to female political leadership in Africa, I am encouraged by the determination of young women to disrupt the status quo.

This is a challenge and call to action that requires both collective and individual commitment.

Work–life balance has been extremely important to me. My daughter left me in London to go and live with her father in Gettysburg, Pennsylvania, when she was thirteen years old. Although it was extremely difficult to agree to, it turned out to be one of the best decisions I ever made. She is my only biological child and therefore my attachment was very strong. As it would mean long stretches of time away from her, I had to make sure that my decision included the flexibility to visit her as often as I needed. We have managed to have a close mother–daughter relationship without me missing significant events in her life, despite living in separate countries. I have also found time to go away on holiday and leave work-related issues behind. This deliberate strategy has helped me manage my physical and psychological wellbeing. I have managed to surpass some of my expectations and I believe the future promises many more opportunities for me to make a difference in the lives of others. I try to make sure that I celebrate my accomplishments whenever I can for a life that has been complex but fulfilling.

1
Childhood

My family

I was born in July 1969 in the village of Foindu Perrie
in the Pujehun District of Sierra Leone. My parents,
Cecilia Kawa and the late Augustine Kamanda, were
also from the Southern Province; from Pujehun and
Bo Districts, respectively. My mother was a business-
woman and my father a Communication Specialist in the Army. My mother is a practising Muslim
and my father was a staunch Catholic. I was raised
in the Catholic faith, which I practised until I moved
to a Methodist secondary school. At birth, a well-
respected Muslim cleric gave me his name, Kamoh
Allieu, because I arrived clutching something in my
tiny hands, which was interpreted as a 'special gift'
of protection for the future. To be named after a man

signified that I would grow up strong with a bright future. People from my village still know me as that special child Kamoh Allieu.

In my formative years I grew up answering to the name Susuewa (Big Susue). I spent them with my mother and maternal grandfather Ama Kawa, an ex-military officer who had fought in the Burma Campaign during the Second World War. I don't remember my grandmother Fodia, nicked named 'Good Food', but I understand she was outspoken, fearless and stylish. However, I do remember my great-aunt Haja Fatmata Sheriff, whom I knew as my grandmother. My grandparents played a very significant role in my life.

All accounts of my first five years suggest that I was a spoiled and demanding little princess. My mother told me stories of my infant years and being a sickly and difficult baby. I thought she was exaggerating until I bumped into a woman from my village who confirmed her stories. I was standing next to my mother during the International Women's Day celebration when the woman asked about Kamoh Allieu. My mother responded, 'This is Kamoh Allieu.' In total amazement, the woman turned to my mother and said, 'You see how I discouraged you from giving her up; now look at her.' I was very shocked at this and asked my mother why she had wanted to give me away. This is what the woman told me:

'You were a very demanding child; you couldn't drink water unless it was from the spring or otherwise you would get sick, sometimes very seriously. Other babies would be fine wetting their nappies two or three times, but if your nappy wasn't changed immediately, the entire village would not sleep because you cried your eyes out. You had to have powder on your neck and shoes on your feet. This was the only time you were happy. It was too much for your poor mother and she used to think you should have been born to some rich woman, not her. She therefore considered giving you up for adoption.'

Another reason my mother might have wanted to give me away was because she had already lost two infants and believed I would die too. I reckon the fact that I did not die in her care should have been a good sign. Later grandpa Ama Kawa changed my name to Susue K Kawa, giving me his surname. Apparently, grandpa Ama's reason was that my father had not followed the proper procedures for his granddaughter to carry the Kamanda name; as a mark of respect, however, I would have the initial K. I was told that Papa was very scared of grandpa Ama. I became one of his favourite grandchildren until his death. This background gave me a clear understanding of why grandpa was so protective of me, but I only learned some of these stories after his death. I am sad not to have engaged my late father on this issue so I could hear his side of the story.

Schooling

I started primary school at the Sierra Leone Church School in Kenema in the Eastern Province. I remember the first couple of years because of my late best friend Rosaline whose mother was Headteacher. A Lebanese boy who liked me was always keen to share his lunch with us, but I would refuse. However, Rosaline would take the food and make me eat it, positioning herself so that we could only talk through her. She made sure everyone, including our parents, knew what was going on. She liked the fact that this boy was shy and anyone who wanted some of his food had to be friends with us. I think Rosaline was already planning a wedding even though I clearly wasn't interested. I still can't believe I was being courted at such an early age.

One vivid memory is of being chosen to present, on behalf of the city, a bouquet of flowers to President Siaka Stevens during a visit to launch the Agricultural Cocoa Show. This was an important event that attracted both national and foreign dignitaries. My mother always dressed me well for school, but as a six-year-old I couldn't understand why that day she needed to put extra grease on my head and face and put me in new shoes and uniform. On the way to the airfield my teacher held my hand at the front of the line until I was pulled aside and handed a bunch of flowers that was bigger than me. I required extra help to walk up to the President who was dark and tall.

I don't remember saying anything because I was in awe. I gaped at him as he bent down, smiled, took the flowers and shook my hand. It was a proud moment for my mother and my school.

At the end of my second year my younger sister and I went to spend the holidays with our father in Freetown, the capital of Sierra Leone. Papa had moved there with our stepmother and brother Junior. As soon as we arrived, Papa named us Naasu I and Naasu II. He also told me that I should be called Naasu Kamanda in school and not Susue K Kawa. Naasu was his mother's name and Papa told us that all his daughters were to be called Naasu. We were to be differentiated by a number and middle name. My younger sister did not seem bothered by the name change. She was also Papa's favourite and looked just like him.

I started attending Murray Town Army Municipal School in class three but didn't like my new environment. The story of the wicked stepmother became my reality. I was used to grandpa Ama doting on me and here I was with a distant father and a stepmother who clearly didn't like me. I lost my princess crown and became a target for beating. My younger sister escaped this treatment. My stepmother wouldn't dare beat her because she was adored by our father. I noticed blatant favouritism towards my siblings. My younger ones received all the attention while I was vilified for 'looking like' my mother. My memory of the school is vague because of what went on at home; I felt like a stranger and didn't feel loved. I tried to bond with Papa during his boot-cleaning routine. He taught me how to shine them using Kiwi polish, a cotton cloth and water. It was only properly done when you could see your reflection in the boots. I was brought up to look after my siblings and do my very best. Papa's lectures were tough, but he always told me that life wasn't easy. My happiest time was when Papa took us to his village to meet our grandmother Naasu during school holidays. I had a totally different experience – it was immediate love.

Grandma Naasu was warm and gentle. Unfortunately, my warrior grandfather passed away before I was born and my stepgrandfather was blind, so couldn't help much with caring for us. Grandma was the queen of her village/island and had tobacco, cotton and rice farms. She liked fishing and hunting for bush meat. I enjoyed all these activities, especially using a mudsling to frighten the birds from the rice farm. Grandma Naasu was always smartly dressed and smoked a tobacco pipe when she was going to the farm. She loved cooking and sang during her daily chores. Holidays with my grandparents remain my best childhood memories.

When Papa's army career ended, he took a job with the Ports Authority. We moved to Congo Water Wellington where I started Wellington Municipal School in class five. Similar to my first primary school, there was a boy who liked me, but his tactics were more aggressive. Papa had already started lecturing me about boys and men, saying that I should never allow any of them to touch me. If a boy touched my stomach it was bad and I should immediately report him. Unfortunately, this boy decided to slap me in school, but instead of reporting him to the teachers, I came home and told my father. We immediately went to his house where the boy's father was sitting on the veranda. We asked for his son and when he came out a little later, Papa took him by his trousers and slapped his bottom a few times. He warned him never to touch his daughter. He even warned the father that if his son ever did it again, he would be held responsible. I knew that Papa meant that, next time, the father rather than the son would receive the beating. I was very proud of my father for standing up for me and told all the girls in my class what had happened.

Another time I remember Papa standing up for me was when one of our neighbours came into the wash yard (outside bathroom) while I was taking a shower. I was surprised and scared because it was in the women's section; he wasn't supposed to be there. I was naked and he looked at me, smiled and left. When Papa came home, I told him what had happened during our usual daily catch-up. He didn't say much, and I continued speaking. A few minutes later when we saw the man returning from work, Papa got up in a manner that I recognised as trouble time. The next thing I remember was Papa hitting the man who immediately soiled himself. I remember the unpleasant smell but I was just so happy that

Papa was looking out for me. He represented security; nothing bad would happen to me when Papa was around.

However, he couldn't protect me from life at home where my stepmother was unhappy with us and our father. There was too much tension at home, and school was my refuge. I was a bright student despite the insecurities at home. I would be sent out to sell huge trayfuls of cakes wearing the infamous blue plastic 'Fullahman Chacha' sandals. In those days you were mocked by your peers for wearing them because they were seen as a sign of poverty and inferiority. It was just one of the ways my stepmother made me look bad. My father could afford nicer sandals, but he always gave in to my stepmother's wishes. Papa did what she wanted. I don't remember ever being praised by Papa, but I remember the countless, merciless beatings for any single mistake I made. Although I was just a child, I was not allowed to make mistakes. As a result, I had no idea what good behaviour was because my life was a constant rebuke. My younger siblings never had to endure what I went through, and I felt like a child caught in a battle between my parents. I did not feel loved or safe. To escape their wrath, I wanted to go to boarding school. My dream came true when I was admitted to St Joseph's Secondary School in Moyamba.

A week prior to my departure for boarding school there were no preparations at home, but I daren't ask what was going on. The nightmare continued until the night before I left. I went to bed crying and at 4am Papa woke me up to go to the bus station. I was numb and wondering how on earth this trip was going to happen. I had no trunk, books, provisions, etc. It felt like I was going to prison, not boarding school. But it wasn't my place to ask, I just had to obey Papa. On our way, Papa said we had to stop by his uncle, my lovely and eloquent grandpa George who was a bus conductor. Although my father had bought all the things I needed for boarding school, he could not bring them home because of my stepmother. I was shocked but I kept my feelings to myself as Papa sounded sorry. Although I looked fine on the outside, inside I was distraught; I just wanted him to disappear from my life. At that moment I hated him with all my being. I cried all the way to Moyamba Junction to meet my mother who was taking me to my new school. I was eleven and burdened with this life of hell.

My mother was happy to see me with everything that I needed; I did not tell her what had happened because it would just end up as the battle of the fittest between her and Papa. She wasn't bothered about my feelings. We got to Moyamba only to find that I had lost my place at the boarding school because the fees had not been paid on time. I would only be admitted in the second term. This meant that I had to spend the first term living with my mother's cousin and his wife who were total strangers. I was so hurt that I still can't remember their names. I was unhappy, counting down the days to becoming a boarder.

Form 1.1 at St Joseph's was an elite stream for the best-performing students across the country. My classmates came from diverse backgrounds, including girls who lived in the United Kingdom. We called these girls 'swen swen' (posh) because of their British accents. Some of our teachers were from Ireland and many, including the principal, were nuns – Cluny Sisters. The senior girls acted as guardians and wonderful, caring substitute mothers and mine was Massah Bomah, the Head Girl. I believe my inspiration to lead got nurtured here. For once, I felt safe and loved by everyone around me. Although I was a day student during the first term, I was happy in school. Once I became a boarder, I wrote Papa a letter to end all letters. I told him that I resented him and wanted nothing more to do with him. My progress in school was excellent, but the girls were very competitive. In boarding school, I experienced love and sisterhood with my friends Cecilia Greene, Josephine Swaray, Bridget Sisay, Sophie Moody and Zainab Mansaray. Although the routine was strict, togetherness and sharing were encouraged. One of my favourite times was going to the stream to do the laundry and to bathe at weekends. During the walk there we bonded and shared secrets, including giggling about meeting the boys from St Michael's, which was forbidden. Our matron was strict but caring and I loved her even when I got into trouble. I dreaded Saturdays when we had to recite endless prayers. I believe that we were being groomed to become nuns. A few of the other girls eventually became nuns and I even considered it.

Siesta time was my happiest moment. It was compulsory and I enjoyed the tranquillity; for once, I felt settled and secure. But my world was about to be turned upside-down.

The school informed our parents at the end of the second term that the boarding school would be closing at the end of the school year. I was confused and upset because my mother told me I would be living with her and my other siblings. She already had two more children as well as my sister. She said that she wanted all of us to live together. I had mixed feelings because, although it would be good to be with her and my siblings, boarding school was my safe space and I was going to leave all my new friends. When we returned to school for the final term we all knew who would move to other girls' boarding schools and who would be leaving the town.

In 1982 I started my second year at the Methodist Secondary School in Kenema. The school was just four years old and a completely different atmosphere. I had come from a competitive stream to being in one that was second best in this school. Although I was demotivated, I quickly realised that I just had to get on with it and do my best. The following year I made it to the green stream, enrolled in the Scripture Union, school debating society, and drama club, and took a keen interest in volleyball. As school represented my safe space, I had to make it work. I was always busy and excelled across the board. In form three, I chose agriculture instead of home economics because I wanted to show the boys that girls could study it too. Only two girls chose agriculture and both of us were clever and we were top of our class. I was also good at extracurricular activities and became popular. My volleyball skills were such that I eventually became school captain, leading our team to win the inter-secondary school and regional championships. I was later selected to be part of the regional team to compete in Freetown for the National Championship trophy, which we won. Academically, I did well and became the head of the school debating society. In fifth form I was appointed to head prefect.

Me, around the age of fifteen, in my school uniform

CHILDHOOD

Despite these successes there were some troubling
times. I lost my best friend to an unsafe abortion and
I was raped. Naturally, this has had a lasting effect on
my psychological wellbeing. In accordance with our
tradition and culture, I also went through my rite of
passage into the Bondo Society.

Rite of passage

As a teen I looked forward to my rite of passage. Not
only because it was mysterious, but also because of
its code of secrecy; not even mothers are allowed to
reveal what is involved. We just saw it as an exciting celebration to mark when girls became women
and enjoyed a new level of respect from the community and their peers. Like many other girls, I looked
forward to it anxiously. When it was time, grandma
Naasu and a few of my mother's aunties came for the
ceremony and accompanied me and my sister into the
bush. The same evening, I went through the initial
rituals, including circumcision. When my blindfold
was eventually removed, the first person I saw was
grandma Naasu. Grandma and other family members
were singing and dancing. I didn't know what to do
or say because I was in pain; I was simply aware of all
the people who loved me looking extremely happy. A
few minutes later grandma Naasu gave me a brief lec-
ture in Mende. She called me Ntorma, which means
'namesake':

'Ntorma, I am so happy today. I am proud
that you have gone through Bondo. I had to
rub what's on your body because I am like
you today and you are like me. You have gone
through the worst pain life can ever throw at
you. You went down as a girl and rose like a
woman; that is resilience. Whenever you find
yourself in difficulties in life, remember this
day and believe that you will rise and conquer.
You are now part of us, we are one, you are a
woman.'

I just stood in silence as my grandma led the large
group of smiling women. They danced around me
and sang loudly and happily about attaining wom-
anhood. I don't remember seeing my mother, but my
grandma Naasu literally tried to obliterate my pain
with this fanfare – she was in charge. Grandma stayed
with us in the bush for six weeks while we healed and
completed all the required rituals. There was a lot of
emphasis on community leadership, fostering sisterhood, caring for family and respect for authority. One
key element was raising our self-esteem as a Bondo
woman. We were constantly told that nobody should
put us down and that the society would always be our
support system in time of need. I was most interested
in the leadership and self-confidence training and I
believed that I was now the same as the older women
in my family. We had no complications during our rite
of passage because in those days practitioners trained

for many years before they acquired the status of an initiator.

Rape

I was subjected to several rape incidents while at secondary school. Unfortunately, the act was so culturally normalised that discussing it with anyone just attracted stigmatisation and victim blaming. The term 'rape' didn't exist in our formal language, although it was well articulated in my first language Mende as 'Kpudemee', meaning forcefully having sex with someone. My perpetrators were trusted men in positions of authority. The first experience was with a religious leader, the Reverend from my church. I was an active member of the Scripture Union and he became fond of me during preparatory classes for confirmation. He praised my intelligence and started giving me roles in church, including reading during church services. Over time I genuinely felt this man, who I regarded as a spiritual leader, liked and cared about my wellbeing. As a child who lived with lots of insecurities at home, it was reassuring to have him believe in me.

The first abuse happened in the church house when he asked me to come into one of the rooms. There was no conversation – just a gentle kiss on my lips. I was very petite, perhaps slightly over 3ft tall, with a man who was over 6ft tall and possibly three times my body weight. The next thing I remembered was my knickers were pulled down and he was trying to force his huge penis into me. It was very painful, but he kept telling me it was OK. After he finished with me, I saw blood; he told me it was probably my period. Going home was scary because I knew I would be in trouble if anyone noticed. It would be me in trouble, not him. Fortunately, my mother was out of town so I managed to avoid been noticed. After that incident he made it a habit to have sex with me at every opportunity, including in the church office. I never told anyone because nobody would have believed me. I would have been blamed and punished for being violated. Unfortunately, I got pregnant – although I did not realise until my mother found out and I was mercilessly beaten. The pregnancy was safely terminated, and despite all the pressure and beating, I never revealed to my mother who the father was.

The second person to rape me a year later was a family member. He was in his forties and a tall, large man. He was a god-like figure and highly respected in the family. When he spoke to you, it felt like a privilege. I spent some of my school holidays with his family; his daughter was only few months older than me. I loved staying with them and used to share a bed with my cousin who was very fond of me and always brought me lovely gifts whenever she returned from London after the school holidays. I idolised her; she was calm, kind and I looked forward to visiting her family.

One day he came to our town on a business trip and the following morning my mother asked me to take some food round to him. The company residence where he was staying was isolated and well protected. When I got there, he was lying on a sofa. After a little while he got up and went into a room. He was wearing white boxers and a vest. I thought perhaps he was going to get me some lunch money or arrange transportation to get me back home. But he opened the door and asked me to bring the pillow from the sofa. I innocently fetched it: there were only the two of us in this huge mansion. Upon entering the room, he calmly shut the door and asked me to sit on the bed. I didn't know what was happening because I didn't connect him to anything bad. He went into the bathroom and then came back and lay down on his stomach. He asked me to scratch his back. When I looked hesitant, he smiled and said it was OK, that I should relax. A few minutes later he pulled me onto the bed and raped my tiny little self. I was in total shock and powerless. He just did what he did quickly and then I left. I can't remember whether he gave me any money to get home. He told me to tell my mother that he would stop by to see her. Later that day when he came round to visit, my mother was so happy. She had no idea what that filthy man had done to her daughter.

Sadly for me, I had to pretend and smile. This man knew nobody would believe me, and his way of keeping me quiet was by being nice to me and then raping me at every opportunity. I dreaded going on holiday to his house. Whenever I was in Freetown he would track me down, sometimes just turning up and saying that he had come to collect me. He was very powerful with strong connections. I had zero chance of escaping him because he was obsessed with me and would get his driver to track me down.

At one point, I believe he wanted people to find out because he became emboldened and would personally track me down while I stayed with relatives. In an attempt to run away from him, I took refuge in my friend's house and started living with her parents. I told my friend and her mother about him, but this man was too powerful. I also realised that most mothers would feel proud if this man was courting their daughter. The problem was that this was sexual abuse and it was something they didn't really understand, but I needed somewhere to stay. The abuse continued until I finally left for London, although he still tried to carry on with his abuse there. By then I was no longer the timid little girl. I told him to stop and reported his behaviour to one of his friends. This friend was aware of what was going on but hadn't realised how I felt about it. Rape is about power, and the two men who raped me were no strangers to me: they were both held in high esteem by others, trusted and powerful. The common currency they shared was my vulnerability as a child and how powerless I was to tell anyone about their deeds. Both of them are now aware that I am no longer that young girl they raped, but a woman with a voice who is speaking up and using her experiences to prevent and protect others from the repulsive act of rape.

Entering adulthood

I enrolled at the West African Methodist Collegiate School to avoid going back to my mother's after the school holidays. The school was affiliated to the Institute of Commercial Management and the registration fee was fourteen pounds sterling. I had no way of paying it, but a family friend from overseas visited Freetown, I was able to contact him and he wrote the cheque for my registration. This was only a temporary relief as I still had to find another eighty pounds for the examination. Almost all of my new classmates were from middle-class backgrounds and weren't facing the same predicament. Nonetheless, I never felt inferior to them and they never once referred to our socio-economic differences. I bonded with my friend Jorbay and instantly became a member of her family. Her father was a Major in the Army and he reminded me of Papa. I started to spend more time with Jorbay. For the first time I began to understand what family life was really like. In 1988, a few months after we started school, almost all the girls took part in the Miss Sierra Leone Beauty Contest. I had already won Miss Kenema in 1986, which made me eligible to represent my city. Unfortunately, none of us made it to the top three, but we were incredibly happy to have participated. I was a popular student even though the collegiate was a boys' school. They used to call me 'Miss Bad' because of my Michael Jackson hairstyle. Unfortunately, I couldn't afford to pay the examination fees so I dropped out. Jorbay left to go to Bournemouth to complete the course and I was back to life's uncertainties. I decided to get a job and found one as a reservations clerk at a leading travel agency.

The majority of my friends had started travelling overseas. My job at the travel agency required me to go to the airport and I started to consider travelling abroad. Although I wasn't desperate, peer pressure got the best of me when one of my remaining friends left. I decided to get a passport and find out what I needed to obtain a visa for the United States. I knew that I needed an invitation letter. In my naivety, I wrote an invitation letter to myself with no other supporting documents and queued for hours at the American Embassy. When I eventually reached the interview desk, the consular officer asked for all the necessary documents. I told him that I didn't have them, but as I could get a ticket through my job, I just needed the visa. My confidence must have amused him because I explained that I wanted to travel because all my friends had gone. He refused to issue a visa but advised me on what was required. But I couldn't think of any family member or friend who would be generous enough to send me overseas. However, simply going to the embassy and getting rejected did the trick. It instantly put me into the category of possible overseas goer. For me that was enough: only the consular officer and I knew that I didn't have the relevant papers. It removed the peer pressure for me to go overseas.

Navigating life as a young adult was pretty much the same as during my late teens. I was used to living life on my own, even though I stayed with family members and friends. I had had to fend for myself since I was seventeen and my job at the travel agency gave me my first taste of independence. I met Mariama who became a big sister and mentor, but our boss wasn't very fond of me and picked on me unnecessarily. Things got so bad that I was reassigned temporarily from the ticketing department to the Spanish Consulate, which was the owner's other business. Although it was a relief, I didn't like it there because I was constantly under the radar of the owner of the company. Also, I didn't understand Spanish. This became a problem when the Spanish Ambassador to Sierra Leone paid a visit. It was instantly obvious that he liked me, but he didn't speak good English. He was the big chief and my boss was trying extremely hard to impress him during his official visit. However, whenever they were in the office the Ambassador would find ways of talking to me, which didn't go down well with my boss. He would smile at the Ambassador, while directing looks of disapproval towards me. It was a rather funny situation because I enjoyed flirting. I left the company when the secretary came back to her job; I didn't want to return to the ticketing department. I was aware that I had become a handful and it wouldn't be long until I was asked to leave. Although I loved my job, I no longer enjoyed the atmosphere; it was time for me to explore other opportunities.

One afternoon I was walking in the main business district when a man came running after me. When he finally caught up with me, he said:

'Me'me boss na e see you wae we dae drive jis nor, na waiteman e say mek ar call you please. Ar tink e lek you.' (My boss saw you while we were driving, he is a white man and he asked me to call you. I think he likes you.)

I instantly rebuked him because it was culturally perceived that only prostitutes dated white men. I was furious that he had the audacity to come and try to pimp me for his boss. But he was very reassuring that this wasn't the case and that his boss had never tried to date any woman in town. He was excited that his boss had shown an interest in someone and even if I didn't like him, it would be nice just to say hello at his lawyer's chambers. Out of courtesy, I accepted and met two very good-looking men.

I had a long-distance relationship with this man and he showed genuine interest in my wellbeing and future. A few months later he sent me a Fiat and suggested I used the car as a hotel taxi to generate an income. As I didn't know how to drive, it was agreed that the driver would run it. However, the driver became controlling and tried to take advantage of the fact that I couldn't drive. He began to cheat me of the earnings. Two months later he sold all the spare parts, including tyres and batteries and telling people that he owned the car. After several failed attempts, I got my cousin to accompany me to retrieve the car from the hotel. Although he resisted in the beginning, the driver succumbed after I threatened to call the police. I told my cousin to teach me how to drive and we started the process immediately. I slowly drove the car home and soon obtained my driving licence. A year later the relationship ended, unrelated to the driver incident, but we still maintain a healthy and long-lasting friendship.

The Civil War had started in 1991, but we were oblivious and never thought it would reach Freetown. Then came the Military Coup in 1992 with all the excitement of the young military rulers. Some were my contemporaries and it felt good to see these young, energetic soldiers. A few were very handsome and pleasant, and I had a friend who I knew before the Coup. This friendship meant I met many of the senior officers in the government, including the head of state. It was strange to see so many young people in charge: we were full of hope for a better country.

Later in 1992 I met a businessman at the airport in Conakry who was visiting Sierra Leone for the first

33

time. He lived in Senegal and we started a relationship. He became very fond of me and invited me to London during one of his trips. In those days we didn't require a visa to go to the United Kingdom, but an older female friend and mentor decided to get me a Schengen visa and encouraged me to visit other places in Europe during my stay. It was interesting how quickly things moved in my life. In January 1993, I landed in London on a cold, frosty morning. I was immaculately dressed in a Michael Jackson jacket. On arrival, the immigration officer questioned me about my visit, but I wasn't worried as I had no intention of staying in Britain. Life was comfortable at home despite the looming war. He asked where my host worked and I told him at the London Council. In Freetown we had the Freetown City Council and I was keen to impress the official. I still remember the expression on his face. He asked me to take a seat and ten minutes later he allowed me to go through. When my friend picked me up, I couldn't understand why he was laughing at my 'London Council' reply. I didn't get the joke. I was in England and I didn't care if I said the wrong thing. Now it does make sense and I can see the funny side of it.

Before I left for London, I visited Papa to share the good news with him. My relationship with him had been severely damaged and I never felt he loved me. I only used to visit him to escape from my mother. He would accuse her of basically the same things he and my stepmother did to me. His house was just one of my many runaway destinations. But Papa apologised to me before I departed for London and explained his behaviour. I forgave him and he told me that he was proud of the woman I was becoming. I had just started loving him again before his sudden death while I was in London. I miss him dearly because I believe he had more to share with me, but we never got the opportunity to get closer. May his soul continue to rest in peace.

2
Marriage, Love and Friendship

Marriage

My teenage and early adult relationships suffered because of my experiences of rape. I didn't trust men – especially those in power. I had a few boyfriends close to my age, but my trust was betrayed by one of them when I was eighteen. It was my first proper relationship and I loved him very much. We met in Freetown; he was handsome and laid-back and I felt he loved me too. We came from different socio-economic backgrounds. His parents were upper-class and affluent; mine were basically working-class and divorced. Nonetheless, we fell in love and his mother, who had a shop on the road where I lived, liked me. I felt truly special when he introduced me to his mother because it showed real commitment even though we were only eighteen and nineteen. He was still at boarding school when we met, and I would travel to visit him and stay in a nearby hostel. He would sneak out of the school to visit me in the evenings. Our love blossomed and I was devastated when he abruptly ended the relationship. I found out later that he fell in love with another girl who was very pretty and whose background was similar to his. I felt hurt and came to the conclusion that he only dumped me because I wasn't from an affluent family. That feeling affected me deeply; I felt betrayed and angry, and resented him.

I eventually moved on and met someone who was about five years older than me, but I wasn't sure I was ready to commit. Although he showed me genuine love and affection, so much so that I introduced him to my mother, I wasn't trusting enough to go deeper. Despite his great qualities, he had a child and his child's mother was very rude. She looked for every opportunity to embarrass him publicly or privately. This was something I seriously disapproved of and it affected my decision not to continue a long-term relationship with him.

While I was in London, the war had escalated and was getting closer to Freetown. When I called my mother to inform her that I was returning, she became furious and warned me that unless I returned in a casket, I shouldn't even think about coming home. I was devastated because I couldn't see myself living in London based on my experience so far during my short stay.

Despite the looming war, I had a comfortable life in Sierra Leone. London was cold, and the people were not as friendly as back home. The thought of telling my current boyfriend, who was residing in Senegal, was also scary; I was going to have to disappoint the first man who truly cared about me. He was also the first man to decide not to have sex with me for a year after I refused his initial advances. He told me that he wanted me to understand that he loved me with or without sex and he proved it. To destroy this relationship for the unknown was unthinkable. I would be betraying his trust. When I finally told him, he was furious. He warned that I would suffer in London because it wouldn't be the same as the life he had introduced me to. He wanted me to return so we could plan how to support me going to university, which was my big dream. My mother's influence was too strong and I reluctantly stayed and jeopardised my relationship. I didn't even have a permanent place to stay until my friend Jorbay rescued me and took me, without telling her sister, to their two-bedroom flat. Although I appreciated her kind gesture, I felt uncomfortable and wanted to return home. She eventually convinced me to stay and wait until the end of the war.

Gradually I began integrating into western culture. I travelled to Belgium and France and started to make my own way in London. I had my fair share of bad treatment by family and friends but eventually found my own place and a job. My jobs included early morning cleaner, chambermaid, picker and packer, and labouring. A friend of mine introduced me to an agency in Earls Court for the picker and packer job. We used to leave home at 4am to report to work at 5am, when we were driven to Greenford near Heathrow for a 12-hour shift. It was a far cry from my lifestyle back in Sierra Leone, even during difficult times, let alone compared to what my boyfriend had introduced me to during our short time together in London. But I endured it and tried to make the best out of the situation because the war back home was intensifying. The reason for staying began to make sense, and I realised I had an opportunity to finally go to university and achieve my dreams. That was the final seal.

During this period, I met a man who I will call 'Ron' in Cumberland Place near Marble Arch. I was visiting a delegation from Sierra Leone who asked me to get some water from the supermarket around the corner. On my way to their flat I saw a Bentley pull over, and a middle-aged Englishman get out and walk towards me. I was wearing a large hooded winter coat and it was freezing. I couldn't imagine anyone would be interested in me. He told me that he had seen me when I came out of the supermarket and had driven around the square to see if he could stop and talk to me. He asked whether it was OK for him to help me with the water because the bottles looked heavy. I reluctantly agreed and he accompanied me to the apartment and we ended up exchanging telephone numbers. I was sharing my first flat with my friend

Helen in Tulse Hill in South London at the time, and when I returned home that night, I told Helen what had happened. She was excited, but I was suspicious of this rather wealthy-looking man trying to court me. It didn't make sense when there were so many beautiful women in London. The following morning he phoned and asked whether he could come to visit me. Helen was looking at me when he called, and her big eyes were urging me not to mess this up. I asked him to come to my rather unimpressive estate in Tulse Hill.

On the Saturday morning he showed up in a brand-new Jeep Cherokee, which only made Helen encourage me to be nice to him. I could see that he wasn't comfortable about the area; he kept going outside to check on his car. I was also worried that his presence in our flat might make us a target for robbery. He invited me to dinner a few days later, picking me up in his Bentley. He took me to a restaurant that I believe was a private members' club. He dropped me off, and a man dressed in black led me to an exclusive area where I waited for Ron. There was just the two of us. I refused to drink any alcohol because I was still somewhat suspicious.

During dinner I told him about moving further out of London to an area with a worse reputation. I told him my rent was already paid and the furniture ordered. He asked whether I would allow him to come and view the flat, as he didn't think it was safe. I agreed and the following day he came round while I waited for my wardrobes to be delivered. He looked so out of place, especially in the lift, which smelled of pee. I didn't like it, but this was my reality as I tried to navigate life as an immigrant. The following day he asked me to meet him in Marylebone in a beautiful one-bedroom basement flat. He told me I could live there rent-free until I sorted myself out. I instantly told him no; I was comfortable with my life. Although the flat was nice, I believed I would have been under his control and he might have made my life miserable. Besides, I was enjoying my freedom. I was not under the sway of anyone. I just wanted to be by myself and then, maybe later, with someone on my own terms. Ron and I remained friends even though I refused to move into the flat. We dated briefly, but I just couldn't trust him. I believe he was someone important who felt safe with my naivety. I always told him exactly how I felt, and he seemed to like me even more and gave me nice gifts. He lived in the country and travelled a lot. I never asked his last name, nor did I request to visit his home as he also owned a beautiful flat in Swiss Cottage. We had a good friendship, but I never fell in love with him.

In 1993 I met my husband at our mutual friends' wedding reception. His friend married my friend and they were preparing to leave for the US. I couldn't attend the wedding because I was in the middle of moving, so I had to get ready for the evening reception at the venue. As I left the bathroom, I saw a man with a goatee beard sitting next to the door. Our eyes met and something told me that this was my future husband. I didn't even know his name let alone his situation; it was a weird experience. As he didn't fit the type of men I was normally interested in, I ignored the thought. About an hour into the event, he asked me for a dance. I still didn't understand what was going on, but the strong feeling that this was my future husband wouldn't go away. It didn't seem possible that he could be the one. By the end of the evening he had asked me out to dinner, and I agreed.

A few weeks later I kept my promise and went round to his home for dinner. He was legally separated and in the middle of divorce proceedings. He apologised for not having proper curtains in his living room, but I hadn't even noticed. As we sat down to eat, my phone rang; it was Helen. She said my 'ex-boyfriend' was in town and was looking for me; he had called her flat several times. After the phone call, I said I had to leave to see my boyfriend because we needed to sort out several issues. Before I left, he asked me for a second date and I promised to come. I went directly to Park Lane to meet Mr Ex-Boyfriend who wasn't happy that I had vanished from his radar. We amicably decided to stay friends to allow me to move on with my life.

A few days later I returned for my second dinner date with my future husband, although that wasn't our status. After a serious discussion we agreed to give the relationship a try. I was worried about being a stepmother, especially after the way I had been treated by my own stepmother. However, I convinced myself that I would treat his two children the way I would have liked to have been treated. Two months after we met he proposed, and we set a date to get engaged. My one request was to go to university; I was already in the process of applying to a nursing course. He was a gentleman and said all the right things. As we prepared to get engaged, he asked me to move in with him so that we could also save money; I was spending more time in his house than my flat. We got engaged as planned, and my family gave him a one-year deadline for the wedding to take place, otherwise I would be removed.

Two months after our engagement, I got pregnant. I was happy because my fiancé had been trying to convince me to have a child. He was worried about being much older than me and wanted to make sure he had time to spend with any future children. My pregnancy felt like a miracle. I had been feeling unwell and went to see the doctor. She gave me a prescription for antibiotics, but as I was about to leave her office, she asked me when I had had my last period. When I replied we both realised that I was two weeks late. She took the prescription back and sent off a pregnancy test. The hospital results would take at least three working days, so I rushed to a shopping centre to buy a pregnancy test. The result was positive, and I was delighted. I kept the test and waited anxiously for my fiancé. When he got home and I told him the news, he wasn't as excited as I expected. Over dinner with his children, we had often discussed the idea of a baby, and his daughter was praying for a sister. Therefore, I was shocked to receive such a lukewarm response. It marked the beginning of a very turbulent period in my life.

Throughout my pregnancy I felt unsupported and alone in the decision-making. I couldn't understand how we were both involved in getting pregnant, and yet I had to bear the burden of choosing whether to keep it or not. My fiancé looked scared. I felt let down but I decided to keep my child. I was twenty-five with two stepchildren who spent more than 50% of their time with us. My circumstances changed overnight: I lost my glow. My body was becoming cumbersome and I felt trapped; and I was also alone in this painful situation. It was too embarrassing to discuss it with any family members as they would say that it was my fault.

At sixteen weeks, I was excited to go for my scan; they would be able to indicate the sex of the baby. I desperately wanted a girl. My fiancé had a work meeting that he couldn't cancel, which meant he was unable to attend, so I went on my own. I could see all the other happy couples, with the men fussing over their pregnant partners. Moments before the nurse called me, my fiancé arrived and we went in together. Although I was angry when it turned out that he had been playing golf instead of being at a work meeting, I was keen for him to be part of the process.

Things didn't change much. Six months into the pregnancy, I started having doubts about getting married. He insisted we get married before the baby was born as he didn't want to have a child out of wedlock. But I didn't want to get married anymore; I became depressed and cried most of the time because I had no one to speak to about my ordeal. My family was very happy that I was getting married – particularly my mother, who was excited that I was expecting her grandchild. I couldn't take that away from her, especially after there were rumours that I would never have a child. I never knew where these rumours came from, nor did I pay them any attention. As an African woman you must endure pain; my initiation rites of passage had groomed me to be resilient, and any decision to back out would bring the family shame. It was a difficult time and I became suicidal. One afternoon while my fiancé was at work, I stood over the banister in my white underwear. I wanted to throw myself over the stairs. Even now I don't know how I stopped myself. It was scary, and the memory still makes me emotional.

During my last trimester, my stress levels increased. Thankfully one of my fiancé's friends came to live with us temporarily and he was very helpful. He would iron my clothes when I got too heavy to do much. As the wedding approached, I became more and more stressed with the arrangements: I wanted to cancel it. In the early hours of 13 April 1995, I started feeling pains and was frequently visiting the toilet. My fiancé joked that I must be going into labour, which just made me mad. As the symptoms were consistent with labour pain, he insisted on taking me to the hospital. Although the nurses said I wasn't ready and should go home, the pain intensified and I went into labour. It lasted for about 26 hours, and my fiancé stayed with me throughout. We welcomed into the world a 5lb 1oz beautiful baby girl whom we had agreed to name after his mother and my grandmother, but we fondly called her JJ. Giving birth was a very painful but joyful experience.

Our wedding was scheduled for the following day and I told my fiancé we had to cancel, but he said we shouldn't because he was so happy. When the doctors came to see me in the evening, I informed them that I was supposed to be getting married the next day. They looked at me in amazement and decided that we could leave in the morning if nothing had changed medically. We were discharged so that I could attend my own wedding. Of course, nobody was expecting the small extra guest, but everyone was happy and pleasantly surprised that we even made it. However, I was so tired I forgot my husband's name during our vows. After the official photos, we went home to rest. We turned up at the reception very late and left after cutting the cake. I still feel like I was a guest at my own wedding.

My husband was an introvert with a gentle outgoing personality. He was nineteen years older than me. He had lived half of his life in England, was settled in his ways, had his own set of friends and was an avid golfer. He was traditional in many ways and ensured that we never lacked anything as a family. His job and golf were an important part of his life and he wouldn't have been such a successful family man without them. I married a man who was still quietly grieving for his mother, but also angry at his failed marriage. He brought this bitterness to our marriage, making it exceptionally difficult for us to make it a success. Despite all this, he was a man committed to his children and enjoyed spending quality time with them. He was a laid-back father who was very indulgent, and he didn't take kindly to anyone rebuking his children.

I felt my marriage was very controlled. My husband had all the resources, and I felt an insignificant part of the decision-making. Most of the time it was easier just to agree with his decisions because his mind was already made up. It would be pointless to challenge anything. I often felt that he believed that the differences in our age and experience were a huge factor; he didn't think I was old enough or experienced enough to take the lead in decision-making. I found this attitude upsetting as it always put me on the defensive, wanting to fight back. I was rarely able to reverse any of his decisions. This controlling attitude undermined our marriage.

Becoming a mother changed my entire life's trajectory and remains my biggest achievement. I struggled in the beginning because JJ was a marathon crier during the night. I know people say that's how it is, but for a woman who never even had a doll to play with, having to cope with two to four hours of non-stop crying certainly tested my resolve in those first two months. One day, she cried so much that I got dressed at 4am and walked out of the house, leaving her with her father. As I walked towards the tube station, I felt unsafe and returned home. Breastfeeding was difficult because she wasn't keen on breast milk. I wasn't used to having painful breasts full of milk that I couldn't dispense. It was a release when she finally stopped breastfeeding.

The decision to have my daughter was momentous. She was, and continues to be, a blessing on so many levels, including dispelling the unfounded rumours about me being barren in my early twenties. I had always said that I wouldn't have children just because of societal pressure, nor did I want to raise a child by myself. Despite the issues in our marriage, I never regretted being a mother. It was the one thing that kept our marriage together.

Motherhood placed checks and balances on my life that no person or situation had ever done. I could no longer take decisions without assessing the impact it would have on my daughter; life stopped revolving around me. I didn't want my daughter to have the childhood I had had, littered with insecurity. I made a commitment to provide the best I could afford and equally not to spoil her. During her formative years, I would rather forego life's luxuries rather than leave her in the care of someone else. I had made a promise to be a different mother from my own. Our childhoods were worlds apart. JJ was born in a developed country with all the advantages that would allow her to live a secure and meaningful life. In comparison, I was born in a village in a developing country where affording the basics was a luxury. My priority was to maximise the opportunities for my daughter so that she could achieve to the best of her abilities. The first year of motherhood was challenging because of the pressure my marriage was under; it was becoming difficult to sustain the relationship. The physical and psychological wellbeing of my daughter was paramount, so I started to consider alternatives, especially for a stay-at-home mother.

Moving to America

Prior to getting married and becoming a mother, I successfully applied for the DV1 Visa Green Card Lottery scheme to resettle in the United States. When my situation changed, I decided to put the process on hold and focus on building my family life. However, our relationship was deteriorating and the thought of bringing my daughter up in this toxic marital atmosphere was unacceptable. I contacted the American Embassy to enquire whether it was possible to reinstate the process. It was, and I was invited to an interview together with my new family, including my stepchildren. My husband subsequently decided to pull out of the process and refused any financial support towards my application. Fortunately, I was able to get a loan from a friend to complete the application for me and my daughter.

In December 1995, when she was just eight months old, we left for New York to complete our green card process. JJ was extremely attached to her father and when we arrived in New York, she became cranky and would only stop crying when I showed her a picture of her father. While we were in New York, my husband, who had not been interested in moving to America, told me he was considering joining us. I had mixed feelings; my intention was to start a new life without him, but my daughter's relationship with him was equally important. I agreed to give our marriage another try. My daughter and I spent most of our time in Maryland with Mariama, who had worked with me at the travel agency, while awaiting my husband's initial visit to discuss our new plans. JJ became extremely fond of Mariama and would cry loudly whenever she left for work. When she returned home, JJ would play and follow her in her walker around the house. She was a happy and easy-going baby, but I was so exhausted emotionally from my marital issues that I was physically unable to do many outdoor activities with her.

My husband requested to be relocated, and a year later we settled in Connecticut. Everything seemed fine; although he travelled a lot, there were positive signs that we could make our marriage work and we discussed counselling options. Quite soon I found out I was pregnant again. I was excited because I didn't want JJ to be my only biological child. But the honeymoon was short-lived, and things started to deteriorate at home. My happiness turned to depression, and during this time I lost the second pregnancy. It was an extremely painful experience that nearly ended my life. From early on in the pregnancy, I noticed my husband's behaviour was similar to the time I was pregnant with JJ. Although I was sad at losing the baby, a part of me accepted that it was possibly for the best. I decided then not to have another child, and a few months later we were transferred to Gettysburg in Pennsylvania.

Gettysburg was a beautiful historic town and I was optimistic about raising my daughter in this community setting. Although I wanted her to have a different childhood from my own, living in the country was one experience I did want her to have. We bought our first home together and I explored the possibility of going back to work when JJ started nursery. I trained as a certified nursing assistant, which would allow me to work in a nursing or care home setting, with elderly people. I was enjoying the transition from full-time mother to working mother, especially chatting to my daughter during the nursery runs. I had never had this type of bonding with my parents and it felt as though I was reliving my childhood through JJ. She was clever and talkative; she would recount everything from school to me in the car and then repeat it when her father returned home. I tried my best to conceal the pain of my marriage from my daughter. I dreaded the thought of divorce and how it might affect her, but my home life became a conduit for turmoil and was rarely peaceful. I found it hard to pretend being happy for my daughter, and the thought of us leaving was scary. But each day it was becoming clearer that the marriage wouldn't work.

Going to university had always been a major goal and I decided to pursue an associate degree in psychology from the Community College. When I was accepted on the course, I thought it might help me cope with my marital troubles. Not earning much meant I was totally dependent on my husband financially. The little funds I earned from my part-time work were used for JJ's nursery fees. Although it was financially difficult, I was extremely pleased to be paying JJ's fees. Her father would contribute as needed. Due to my husband's income I wasn't eligible for financial aid to commence my associate programme and I couldn't access student loans without a joint application; I knew this would be a difficult conversation. Nonetheless, I explained that our daughter was four and I would need his support to return to higher education. I was shocked to learn that his priority was to have more children since he was getting on in years. My response was that if he didn't provide the support, I would have no other choice but to return to London to go to university. Knowing how financially and academically weak I was, he gave me an ultimatum to either stay and work on our marriage or he would divorce me. Money was for paying bills, not for my education. To his utter surprise I chose education and divorce over the marriage.

The decision to return to London meant recasting several relationships. I was also removing my daughter from an environment she had been comfortable with since she was a baby. I was unsure what the psychological impact on her would be, including not living permanently with her father. Nonetheless, I was optimistic that our new life would provide better opportunities, and we would both adjust accordingly while trying to maintain maximum contact with her father. Legally separating from my husband also meant that we were both free to develop new relationships. I was worried about my daughter's reaction to new people coming into her parents' lives. I would go on to meet two people in my life and JJ was happy with one of these long-term relationships because I had primary custody. I also made it very clear in these relationships that my daughter had a father and didn't need another. This clarity meant there could be a healthy relationship between my daughter and other people in my life. Our transition was well managed with minimal effect on relationships.

It was important for me that both parents were fully involved in the upbringing of my daughter. Our temporary legal arrangement was that I would have custody during term time and her father would make sure that she stayed with him during school holidays. This arrangement was well respected and helped our daughter to settle well. She looked forward to seeing her father and would be counting the days to her holidays because of all the exciting things they did together. Considering the impact my parents' separation had on my own development, safeguarding my daughter from traumatic experiences was a priority. My estranged husband was 100% involved in our daughter's life. All decisions were discussed, and we would jointly agree on what was best for her. However, sending her to private school was contentious because her father was worried that his other children hadn't had the same opportunity. As my only biological child, I was determined not to deprive her of the best educational prospects. Despite the challenges, she attended private school and her father made his contributions through child support.

As a stepmother to two children, I experienced first-hand the negative impact suffered by children who were caught up in difficult parental disputes. Both my husband and I took great pains to avoid such situations. Fortunately, our daughter has grown up knowing both of us individually in our own right.

Despite all the hurdles in our marriage, I couldn't have asked for a better father and ex-husband. He continues to be very supportive of my endeavours and contributes financially when needed. I had my own extended family pressures which made our situation very tense, for which I apologised during our divorce. I believe our age gap and lived experiences also contributed to the different ways in which we viewed life and marriage. We have maintained a well-balanced relationship and remained a close family unit in supporting our daughter.

3
Going It Alone

A health crisis

The final straw was when I collapsed with my four-year-old in the house. I was feeling acute stress at being trapped in my marriage because I had no skills to fall back on. The thought of leaving was daunting, even though I knew it was my only option. We were upstairs in our bedroom and I went to the kitchen to fix some food for JJ. As I left, I remember my little girl asking, 'Mummy, are you OK?' She had been trained what to do in an emergency both at home and at her nursery and thankfully it came in handy. She called the ambulance. I could faintly hear her telling them that her mummy wasn't speaking and was on the floor. I wasn't responding. Fortunately, she followed all the instructions until they arrived, and she let the paramedics into the house. We were both taken to the hospital. At the age of twenty-nine I had almost suffered a stroke.

The follow-up consultation with my doctor marked the farewell to my marriage. I was inconsolable and told the doctor that despite my insecurities, including uprooting my daughter from her comfort zone, being alive was the better option. It was time to return to London with JJ. Fortunately, our tax returns had just been processed, with refunds credited to our joint account. All I needed was money to buy our tickets and some spending money. My husband was on a business trip in California and I wanted to sort everything out before he returned. Unfortunately for me, he was tipped off. I found a Sheriff at my door with a restraining order not to take our daughter out of the country. I was also summoned to appear in court but I managed to get a good, understanding lawyer. I was granted permission to take JJ away temporarily and return for a proper custody hearing. I was relieved to have clearance to travel.

I had lost a lot of weight by the time I arrived in London and was suffering from high levels of anxiety. My eyes couldn't stand daylight and I needed to be in the dark. My journeys were between my bed, sofa and the toilet. I ate so little that it felt as though my body was wasting away. I weighed just 6 stones, the bones in my back were protruding and my face was gaunt. Despite everything, I was determined to get better and turn my life around. I knew that lying down all day and crying wasn't the answer to my problems. I needed to take some tough decisions, including divorce, furthering my education and living the life I wanted. My frame of mind and appearance weren't conducive to going out to parties or nightclubs, but I needed to connect with people. As internet dating didn't exist in those days, I turned to chatlines and dating agencies. Although this is culturally unacceptable, it was something I could do for myself. I needed to regain my confidence to start dating again. It was also a welcome distraction from lying down all day.

Using chatlines can become addictive; you are in your own home and can speak anonymously to lots of people. It was also expensive and racked up my phone bills. But it was a solution to a problem, and fortunately for me, I made a good friend straightaway. He became one of the people closest to me and I always referred to him as my saviour. For the purpose of this book, I'll call him my 'Prince of Foindu' because his name for me was 'Princess of Foindu', the village of my birth. We immediately connected, and this reignited my life. When we met in person, we just fell in love. We had similar backgrounds and could spend hours talking without being bored. He helped me to get up and get going. I applied to an access course at Newham College to prepare for university. The Prince of Foindu became my cheerleader and motivated me to pursue higher education. He bought me a BMW and pampered me with lots of expensive treats. This fairy tale ended sooner than I expected when I was at college. Nonetheless, it was just what I needed to embark on my next chapter. I got back my confidence and was ready to take charge of my life.

Security

I needed purpose and resolve to move my life forward. A committed relationship was high on my agenda, in spite of what had happened with the Prince of Foindu and my looming divorce. I knew the type of person I wanted in my life and I embarked on finding him. One weekend I bought *The Sunday Times*; in one of their columns they had adverts for dating agencies. I knew this move would have been frowned upon in the African community, but I was very impressed with one of the organisations – the Executive Club. The following morning, I phoned them for more information. The lady was very pleasant and explained the background to me. It was a very expensive agency, but I was prepared to make the financial sacrifice to get want I wanted. She invited me to an interview to see whether I was eligible to be on their books. A week later, I went through the application process and gambled my last £750 to register. I was a single parent preparing to go through a divorce, awaiting approval to buy my council property, with school fees to pay and with many more pressing problems that needed this money. However, my sense of purpose was unshakeable, and I was confident that this would prove a good investment.

As part of my membership, I received the profiles of eight members each week, without photos, and I could attend social events that would improve my prospects of connecting with more people. The criteria for membership were very strict and I was pleased with their vetting procedures. I received my weekly list by mail and if I was interested in a profile, I would inform the club accordingly. I never even used this facility as I met 'Pettle' after just three dates – one with a lawyer, one with a businessman and one with a banker. He was fifty years old and a senior telecommunications executive. A few days later, I called Pettle and we spoke for over two hours. When we met for dinner, we both decided to suspend our membership from the dating agency to pursue an exclusive relationship.

Pettle and I were together for nearly five years. He was my soulmate and extremely supportive of my goals, and we became each other's counsellor in coping with our respective struggles. He became a pillar of strength in my life and guided me through some critical stages that restored my stability and self-esteem. Through his love and support, I bought my first home and later went on to own two more. I attained both my undergraduate and postgraduate degrees. I was his first African girlfriend and he became very interested in my culture, travelling with me to Sierra Leone in 2003 for my undergraduate research project. Although we were both Christians, we had some major differences in practice, but we both respected these differences without any pressure to choose one or the other. Both our families were welcoming and my daughter got along extremely well with him.

I was pleased with my £750 investment to join the Executive Club; I am not sure how my life would have turned out without it. I obtained everything I wanted and more from that single decision, and I continue to reap the rewards.

Divorce

In 2002, I initiated divorce proceedings as soon as I had started on my undergraduate course. It was a tricky decision because the case was filed in Gettysburg and I was required to attend the hearings. All I wanted was the legal dissolution of the marriage; I wasn't interested in any financial benefits. My freedom was paramount because I knew there was a possibility of being held hostage by the process. My lawyers agreed to represent me on a payment plan because I had no money. All I wanted was a smooth process that wasn't detrimental to my studies or our daughter's wellbeing, so someone had to make sacrifices to enable a quick resolution. I recommended that the lawyers speak to each other and get back to me. As far as I was concerned, freedom would offer me more in future opportunities than what I might receive from fighting over the divorce settlement. When the lawyers informed me of my husband's proposal, to their surprise I accepted immediately. I knew I was entitled to more, but I wanted the decree absolute. I turned down any alimony while I waited for the conclusion of the case. I was psychologically divorcing from everything about the marriage except my daughter.

There were a few hiccups regarding custody arrangements. I vigorously fought for primary custody because it was in the best interest of our daughter. I wanted her to have an upbringing during her formative years that she could rely on throughout her life. However, I understood the resistance from my husband. Father and daughter had a special bond and he was going to genuinely miss her. There was no intention on my part to deprive either of them of their strong relationship. My primary goal was to keep that relationship as close as possible. JJ was used to her father not being at home because he travelled for work; we also went away for long periods. Once we had agreed the final details of our daughter's welfare and I was satisfied, I gave my approval. Our marriage was amicably dissolved in 2004, just after I graduated from university. This was the end of an era and marked the beginning of a new dawn.

Spotting opportunities

My flat wasn't in a particularly desirable part of London and people looked down on the area. However, once I realised that I would be paying more in rent than a mortgage, I thought about buying. My prospects were pretty slim because I was commencing full-time study and I wasn't sure that the banks would give me a loan. Nonetheless, once I obtained the right to buy I got a mortgage with additional funds for renovations; the equity on the property was substantial. Despite this extra funding, my mortgage repayments were less than the rent had been and were affordable on my student loan. I officially became a homeowner and was over the moon at this opportunity to get on the property ladder.

I wanted my daughter to attend a better school than those available in the borough and I managed to secure a place at the Ilford Ursuline Preparatory School, a small Catholic independent school for girls. It meant getting up very early during term time so that I could drop her off and catch the train to central London for my lectures. It was exhausting for both of us and I started contemplating moving closer to her school. Fortunately, Pettle had invested in a property next to her school which made life a lot easier for us. Three years later we bought each other's flats, which put me into the private property bracket. It was a huge boost for me to own a semi-detached Edwardian house in a beautiful area.

Business

In 2005 I established Jemna International Limited. Although I had worked hard to attain my dream of higher education, I quickly learned that the job market wasn't so kind to mature students with no professional experience. At thirty-five I was expected to have a solid career history but I realised that I didn't want the insecurity of my position to affect my new-found confidence. Creating my own job and doing something that I liked would give me the work–life balance I envisaged. Setting up a limited company meant I could work as an international development consultant, real estate investor and run a hair and beauty business.

My business interests grew after completing my post-graduate degree. I had more time to explore further opportunities. I had always spent a considerable amount of money on my hair – hair extensions and related products and services. Although I had zero background in it, I knew it was a trillion-dollar industry with huge growth potential. I embarked on an expensive three-day course in the application of hair extensions. The new pre-bonded hair extensions were a smart but expensive alternative to weaving and had attracted millions of women, including me. After I had paid £950 to fix half a head of my hair in a north London salon, I decided to undertake the £1,500 course. At the end of it, I received a certificate and a business start-up package that included tools and sample hair.

Armed with this new skill, I went on the internet to look for hair extension manufacturers. I had spotted a gap during my training course and realised that sourcing products directly, instead of buying them from the salon where I trained, would be more profitable. However, as there were attractively packaged bad-quality products flooding the market in London, it could be a risky venture. My market research showed that Eastern European women were the biggest service users in the market, and they were paying top prices for good-quality products. Fortunately, I came across a company in Los Angeles called Hair & Compounds (H&C) and contacted them. Their business profile and strategy were aligned with my concept and after speaking to the owners, I agreed to do business with them. H&C also had brand recognition because of their high-profile A-list customers in the Hollywood film and music industry.

I was excited to start my new business venture and established Bespoke Hair Extensions (BHEX) under Jemna International UK, renting a small retail space in South Woodford Arcade. Hair relaxer was a huge market for African and Afro-Caribbean women. To operate this business successfully, I needed a full-service salon. I was able to employ my former hairdresser who was leaving her job in an upmarket salon because of childcare constraints. It was perfect timing and a win–win situation for both of us. She was a qualified hairdresser and understood salon management; I was good at sourcing incredible niche opportunities. She was happy to come and work with me on a self-employed basis. As she was very knowledgeable about hair products, she could advise on the various brands. We decided to use Mizani and Avlon in the shop – two of the top products. I contacted their main distributors in London and after they came to inspect our premises, BHEX was approved to carry these two premier lines. This was a brilliant coup for a small start-up business.

A month after BHEX opened, I flew to Los Angeles to meet with two hair extension manufacturers. It was my first visit to California, and I was excited about seeing the real Hollywood. I stayed at the Beverly Hilton and was amazed at the glitz and glamour. It was close to many interesting places I hoped to visit during my stay. The two businesses, Extensions Plus and H&C, were exactly as marketed; I was particularly impressed with H&C because they gave me a tour of their exclusive production facility and I saw first-hand how they processed the products I was buying. They were privately owned and were extremely selective about businesses that carried their brand. They appreciated customers understanding the ethos behind the business and regarded them as part of their family. This mutual ownership model was working well and explained their success despite the high prices they charged. I signed my contract and placed orders with both companies. Everything was set.

Before returning to London, I saw an opportunity I knew would be worth pursuing. I was a Hilton Honours member and earned miles from my frequent Virgin Atlantic flights. With nothing to lose, I contacted the corporate offices of Hilton Hotels about travel packages. I wanted to operate a combined travel and accommodation business exclusively with Virgin and Hilton where I would operate both services through group discounts for ten or more people. The Sales Director was enthusiastic and provided me with both advice and encouragement to pursue this business model. Unfortunately, this business never materialised. I returned to London to run my business full-time and BHEX became well known as an exclusive hair extension salon in South Woodford and beyond. Although the customer base grew, I wanted to remain small to maintain the quality of our service delivery.

Although I had embarked on entrepreneurship, I also wanted experience in my academic fields of study. I knew getting a job wasn't going to be easy because I lacked a solid CV. Volunteering was a good strategy to get into the job market; I applied to a few international development organisations and seized an opportunity with Oxfam GB a few months after completing my postgraduate degree from the Institute of Education. Oxfam was embarking on expanding diversity and inclusion to its trading division for shop managers in the UK. The role of diversity consultant in the trading department was an excellent entry point. Although I wasn't paid, my travel expenses were reimbursed. The training took place in Oxford, but my role was flexible, allowing me to work from home. I visited shops in London and went to the Oxford head office several times a month. This job was a huge boost to me. While working for Oxfam, I also worked one day a week as an associate psychologist at ACE under the supervision of a chartered counselling psychologist. After two years at Oxfam I landed a paid role as a diversity and communications consultant with an education agency.

JJ returns to America

My daughter was doing incredibly well at school. She won a scholarship at primary school after scoring highest during Year Two Standard Assessment Tests (SATs). This reduced some of my financial burden and freed up funds for extra activities, including piano and saxophone lessons. My professional and private lives were perfectly balanced, allowing me to be a full-time mother. This was exactly how I wanted my life to be: spending more time with my daughter and being available to attend all school-related matters. I never missed a single event in her academic or social activities. In Year Six JJ became head prefect of her school.

JJ sat her Year Six SATs for secondary school and we accepted a place at the City of London School for Girls. She finally got the independence she had craved so long for and would travel from Ilford to St Paul's by train. She spent a year at this school, but decided she wanted to study in the US. I wasn't happy about this, especially as she was approaching puberty, but she wasn't happy at her new school. When I told her principal, she encouraged me to allow my daughter to go; her place would be available for two years if things didn't work out in America. That reassurance helped me to release JJ on the understanding that she would return after completing middle school in Gettysburg. It turned out to be one of the most difficult but successful decisions I ever had to take on her behalf.

JJ's move to the US left a huge gap in my life in London, but I decided to accept my empty nest and explore new opportunities. I was in my prime, with plenty to be proud of: a home, business, a beautiful Porsche and a healthy social life. In order to get the best out of the situation, I readjusted my life and decided to sell my main home and rent a place near my business. After a year I realised it was too far away for my new social life and moved to Chelsea. This idea came to fruition when I secured a consultancy job with the Qualifications and Curriculum Authority (QCA) through an agency. As an independent contractor working in customer relations and diversity, I was suddenly earning a substantial weekly amount and could even afford to pay the monthly rent for my studio flat in Chelsea Cloisters with a week's pay. I had disposable income and didn't need to take money from my hair business. My social life was booming, and living in Chelsea suited me perfectly.

I planned my social life as a single woman by joining an exclusive private members' club. I enjoyed going out on my own but I didn't want to be roaming from one nightclub to the other. I joined the exclusive 50 St James's Club in Mayfair which included two restaurants, a bar and one of London's top nightclubs. The clientele was diverse, but mostly wealthy and professional. I was pleased to have invested in becoming a member as it was an excellent conduit for networking.

One evening in 2007, I unexpectedly met Baroness Valerie Amos. We started talking and agreed to keep in touch, and later met for a drink. During our meeting I discovered who she was, and I nearly fell out of my chair. I was so impressed. After telling her about my life, she told that me she had visited Sierra Leone twice. During her visit as International Development Secretary, she had been extremely impressed by Sierra Leonean women. She spoke passionately about our female politicians; how vibrant they were and what a shame it was about the Civil War. When she suggested that I should return home to support post-war reconstruction, it felt as though she had dropped a bombshell.

If a white woman had said this to me, I would have instantly accused her of racism: I was genuinely shocked at her suggestion to go home. I just could not fathom the thought, let alone summon up the bravery, to return to a country that had emerged just five years earlier from a brutal civil war. I was wondering whether Valerie liked me, but I could see she did from her attitude and words. I just couldn't accept the idea;

it made no sense to me. I was speechless, but I do not think she expected a reply: she simply wanted to open my mind to the idea. Fortunately for me, someone Valerie knew walked by our table.

After that evening, Valerie and I stayed in touch. I promised to seriously consider her advice and would keep her posted. Given that JJ was no longer living with me, returning home could prove to be a rewarding option.

In 2008 the financial crisis started to threaten my business investments. The QCA was due to move to Coventry in 2009, which meant my contract was ending. I was also missing having my daughter with me. I started to think seriously about Valerie's advice about returning to Sierra Leone. Part of my divorce settlement was invested in a real estate project in Sierra Leone; it would be good to complete it. I could also expand my salon and hair extension business back home. My plan was to use my limited funds to develop a hair salon franchise in Sierra Leone and finish the apartment complex. This decision would require some compromises, including building a better post-divorce relationship with my ex-husband. His support by taking over custody of our daughter deserves praise, even though I found it extremely difficult to accept. In the end, the freedom it gave me opened up new opportunities.

4
Education

Getting your agency back

Attaining higher education was always my biggest dream. Despite promising academic prospects, this wasn't an option for me because my parents couldn't afford it. Neither of them had university degrees, although my father was fortunate enough to study signal communications in the United Kingdom when he was in the Sierra Leone Army. I found out recently that Papa studied at Sandhurst and became one of the Army's best specialists. I do remember clearly that he spoke and wrote very well; his handwriting was exceptionally neat. Although my parents couldn't afford it, they believed in a university education and prayed that one day I might attend. I was determined to break through the barrier; not just for me but also for my younger siblings. Education was my crusade, and I was out to get it whatever the cost.

Moving to London in 1993 gave me hope of fulfilling my education dream. It became even more pressing when I visited Sierra Leone during the war in 1998 with my then three-year-old daughter and met an old school friend from secondary school. Sophie was already at university. I was proud of her but it also made me feel inadequate, especially as I wasn't happy in my marriage. It was a feeling I never wanted to experience again and it reignited my desire to pursue my dream. Although I didn't show it, I was upset that a classmate from form one was now ahead of me academically: our school had expected all of us to succeed.

When I returned to the US, I shared this encounter with my husband. He told me that I could get all the stability I needed from a second child and his hard work in supporting the family. Of course he was already supporting us, but it didn't address the real issue and the impact on my self-esteem. The thought of having to depend on him forever was troubling and I totally rejected this option. I started exploring alternatives. Although I was accepted to a community college in Gettysburg, it was impossible to fund the course without my husband's support. When I told him about it, I couldn't change his mind. After a heated argument I gave him an ultimatum: either he supported my quest for higher education, or I would move back to London to pursue it. His response was to threaten me with divorce. This motivated and emboldened me to move on with my studies.

Back in London in 2000, I enrolled on an Access to Higher Education Course certificate at Newham College of Higher Education in preparation for university. Life wasn't easy: I was a single mother, having separated from my husband, fighting for custody of my daughter and studying full-time. Money was tight and for a year I was able to receive benefits while I studied. I was determined. Apart from the core subjects I studied counselling, which I found extremely helpful in my situation. I also found computer studies fascinating and remember two specific classes; one learning about the motherboard and the other, more practical, about setting up emails. Having my first email account and learning how to compose and reply to emails felt like winning the lottery. I could feel my confidence increase. My experience as a stepchild, and subsequently a stepmother, influenced the topic of my final project: the challenges of stepparenting. I graduated as one of the top students from the access course and received an award for outstanding performance.

Applying to university through UCAS felt like a dream; I couldn't believe this was finally happening. I chose to study psychology because I wanted to become a chartered counselling psychologist. I applied to various universities in London, but my top choices were UCL and the University of Westminster.

I was accepted by the University of Westminster to read a BSc (Hons) in Psychology. The opportunity was mind-blowing, and I had an immediate cognitive shift regarding my divorce. All I wanted was the opportunity to get an education so that I could be independent. In September 2001, after dropping my daughter off at school, I arrived at the Regent Street campus as a mature thirty-one-year-old student reading psychology. JJ was happy because I couldn't stop talking about starting university. When I received my student card, the emotion hit me and I broke down in tears. This was the moment I had dreamt of and struggled to reach. I had chosen education over marriage and material comforts, and yet I wasn't prepared for this reaction. This was my big-deal moment, and my fellow students rallied around me.

At first, I felt intimidated as a mature woman among young nineteen-year-old students, but I gradually adapted. While the counselling course had introduced me to key psychological concepts, nothing had prepared me for quantitative research methods. This was a core module that I had to pass to progress through the course. Even at secondary school mathematics would make me anxious and I would run away from statistics at the first opportunity. I would have to face this phobia head-on if I were to achieve my dream of a degree. Thankfully, there was extra support and even though I remember telling my course tutor that I would have to drop out because of it, he disagreed; his encouragement helped me to succeed.

Later I was elected course representative. This position boosted my confidence and gave me the opportunity to interact with lecturers and students. As a result, I met three women who became my best friends at university: Lena, Michelle and Carina. We supported each other both academically and emotionally, especially as we were all mature students. These women, and Lena in particular, were always there for me. The divorce proceedings were taking their toll; my second year in particular was difficult, and I performed slightly below expectation. Education became my coping mechanism. Rather than let the divorce affect me, I turned the tables and studied even harder. I reiterated my position with my lawyers; they were to proceed with the easiest options even if it meant walking away with nothing except my divorce absolute. I knew that education would give me access to everything I needed in life, including financial independence. When I realised that the divorce proceedings could be deferred, I decided not to attend any court appearance in my final year so that I could mentally block out my divorce. It allowed me to focus totally on my final year and achieve the best results.

I was surprised at the improvement in my grades after this decision. I scored the highest in my final year and was awarded a distinction in my dissertation, 'A psychological perspective: Investigating the meaning of female circumcision within the context of the Bondo Society amongst Sierra Leonean women'. I also received a first in my applied work experience in a psychological setting. The module I was so afraid of, Research Methods, surprisingly became one of my best modules. I regularly scored above 62%. In 2004 I graduated with an Upper Second Class (Hons) in Psychology. I was thirty-four and divorced. This significant milestone was the second rite of passage in my life.

Master's degree

My daughter was still in primary school when I graduated from Westminster University. As I didn't want to interrupt her routine, I decided to continue with a Master's degree. But I was worried about the financial implications. I had managed to complete my undergraduate studies with student loans, but this wasn't possible for a postgraduate degree. The only options were scholarships, self-funding or bank loans. I consulted my boyfriend Pettle, who advised me to get some work experience first. This was sound advice, but I was worried about losing momentum in pursuit of my academic goals. I told him that I would apply and then make a final decision after I heard back from the universities.

I initially applied for a fully funded doctoral degree in educational psychology, as this was a career path I wanted to continue in. However, a chance meeting with Kona, an old friend, at the Sierra Leone High Commission in London changed my mind. She suggested looking into the subject of gender. She was deeply passionate about it and encouraged me to do some research. In 2005, all I knew about gender was that it tended to involve angry feminists. I even believed they were men-haters who were just out to cause trouble. My ignorance was fuelled by these strongly held beliefs. I couldn't see how the subject fitted in with my cultural values, but I listened carefully to her arguments and realised that I hadn't really done any independent research or read much about gender or feminism. I was simply influenced by the usual stereotypical prejudices. Kona explained what gender studies involved and its potential to change lives. I realised that this was something that might be of benefit if I wanted to work for international organisations. She advised that being at the heart of the growing gender movement in Africa would be a good educational investment and I should strongly consider it. After her brilliant pitch, I promised to look into it and see if any universities were offering this subject.

There were several universities offering gender courses. The University of Sussex and the Institute of Education (IOE) stood out, but I preferred the combination offered at IOE – one of the world's most prestigious institutions in the field of education – and applied. When IOE offered me a place, I was over the moon. I accepted the offer immediately and applied for a bank loan to fund it.

The course at IOE focused on four key areas: Learning Education and Development; Gender, Education and Development; Gender – Theory and Practice in Education; Learners, Learning and Teaching in the Context of Education for All. Because I wanted to continue specialising as a psychologist with a view to becoming chartered, I was assigned a senior psychologist as one of my course supervisors. This ensured my analyses were congruent with the discipline. I was also interested in the education and development modules; despite the heavy theoretical concepts, they were practical. I could see their relevance and the impact they might have on my country and continent. Our class resembled the United Nations, with experts from different disciplines from all over the world. Age wasn't an issue as I was probably one of the youngest in the class. I looked forward to the lectures.

My biggest challenge was the gender classes. I was worried about my biased views and how they might affect my learning outcomes. The first class simply confirmed my biases – it comprised mostly women and I sensed a strong lesbian presence. At first I didn't think I could fit in because I didn't understand most of the discussions. Many of the women in the class had a strong background in feminism, or at least what I considered western feminism. I stayed quiet and tried to remove my biased lenses and learn – this was why I was there, to challenge myself and deal with any prejudices. Although the women were expressing strong views, they didn't appear angry. In fact, one woman I became very close to was proud of being lesbian. She was a gentle person who helped me understand the different concepts. She was so open and comfortable with her life; what I learned from her broke down my prejudices and helped me feel at ease and confident in class.

Part of the course involved a visit to the UNESCO Headquarters in Paris. We had to share rooms and I was paired with my new lesbian friend. We joked about it being a set-up and the others were teasing me that it was a sign for me to give women a go. It was all done in a spirit of fun and I had no worries during the three nights we spent together, even if she did keep admiring my hips. One of the senior officers at UNESCO was impressed with my degree combination, especially Psychology and International Development. As my background was rare in the field, he encouraged me to look for work with international organisations, including UNESCO. However, I told him these big organisations didn't interest me as I had discovered during my course that much of the funding went on administration rather than on direct beneficiaries. He did try to change my mind and I promised to consider his advice.

I decided to undertake my research in Sierra Leone because the Civil War had just ended and it was a good opportunity to collect primary data. My dissertation was entitled 'The Gender Impact of Educational Displacement during Sierra Leone's Civil War (1991–2002): A case study of St Joseph's Vocational Secondary School Moyamba, Sierra Leone'.

I found the research particularly challenging because St Joseph's was where I had spent my first year at boarding school, and I had happy memories. To discover the level of disruption and danger the school had faced during the Civil War, including the rape of students and teachers, was harrowing. I was privileged to be able to collect this vital information for my dissertation. I graduated in 2005, having successfully fulfilled all the requirements for an MA in Education, Gender and International Development from the School of Educational Foundations and Policy Studies – Institute of Education, University of London.

A decade after reading for a Master's degree, I was still contemplating a professional doctorate in counselling psychology. My work in international development had reaffirmed the need and urgency for this specialism because of a lack of experts in this field. If there was an area where psychologists were undoubtedly needed it was in the field of international development. I knew it would require a longer absence, which would have been challenging at the time because of my ongoing work in Sierra Leone. But I continued to keep these thoughts in mind. In 2013 I hosted a professor from Harvard Kennedy School of Government who was in Sierra Leone actively trying to recruit professionals at middle- and senior-management levels.

I was flattered at the opportunity, but the timing was not right. I was only a year into an important new role in the government and leading policy development on gender equality and women's empowerment.

In 2016 a young woman called Aminata emailed me a link, encouraging me to apply for an Oprah Winfrey Scholarship for an Executive Master of Public Administration (EMPA) jointly at NYU and UCL. I told her that as I was approaching fifty I didn't think I had the energy to pursue an intensive course of study. But she persisted with her reasons for suggesting it to me. Above all, she said, I would be an Oprah Winfrey Scholar. This reminded me of my limited contact with Oprah nearly sixteen years earlier and of the time my daughter accused me of not knowing how to read and write because all I did was watch Oprah. Perhaps this was the perfect opportunity to redeem myself by becoming an Oprah scholar. With this extra incentive, I applied for the course. My contract with the government had ended; I was still awaiting re-appointment and considering other options. I also began applying to Harvard University.

The EMPA was more appealing to me because it meant spending the second semester at UCL. In March 2017, I received an email from UCL inviting me to an interview a week later. This was a key requirement since I would be specialising in Global Public Policy and Management, which came under their purview. Luckily, I was already in London preparing to return to Sierra Leone. I was extremely nervous at my interview with Professor Weale and he immediately noticed my anxiety. I told him I was worried about my age, but he reassured me that my age was an advantage because the course was designed for mature candidates. I was optimistic and hopeful that the interview had gone well, although I knew there was a great deal of competition from candidates from all over the world. Professor Weale also informed me about the Pentland Scholarship, which was aimed specifically at global public policy leaders and would require another interview if I was successful in applying. UCL would send me further information about it. Later in March, I received official notification from NYU that I had been admitted to the Robert F Wagner School of Public Service. My excitement quickly evaporated when I realised that I had missed out on the Oprah Winfrey Scholarship. I immediately decided to apply for the Pentland Scholarship because it would be impossible to do the course without a scholarship.

The Pentland Scholarship interview took place in early May; a week later they notified me that I had been awarded the scholarship, which enabled me to take my place on the EMPA at NYU and UCL. I received the decision the night I arrived in Philadelphia to attend my daughter's graduation from Temple University, so it was a double celebration. In August 2017 I officially commenced the course. Being able to attend two such globally prestigious schools was a humbling experience. I was new to the American way of study and, having been out of education for over a decade, I knew it would require some serious adjustments. As I was determined to do well, I spent most of my time in the library making sure I met the course requirements. My cohort ranged between the ages of thirty and sixty years and consisted of top professionals with extensive careers. These included doctors, lawyers and bankers. I found NYU, especially the Robert F Wagner School, a very conducive and enabling environment for learning. It was totally different from the hierarchical structures I was used to within the Sierra Leonean and British education systems.

Accommodation was a problem because I was living a long way from the university and it was costing me more than I could afford. Some weeks, I would stay in an Airbnb, but this was not sustainable either. In the end, my friend Chernor and his wife Assiatou offered me a room in their home, which was nearer to the university. I spent the last two months of the term with them and their boys; it made all the difference in gaining exceptional grades. I also found staying with them therapeutic as I was battling severe depression at the time. This was due to the constant reminder of my ordeal as a rape survivor following the surge of reporting on sexual violence sparked by the #MeToo movement. Spending time off campus, especially with their little boys, gave me a sense of family and purpose, a distraction from the constant bombardment in the news. I finally concluded the NYU portion of my course and headed to UCL for semester two.

London is my second home, so everything was familiar, including UCL, which is one of the oldest and most prestigious universities in the world. Pentland Scholars have the opportunity to meet the Chairman of the Pentland Group, Stephen Rubin, at least once during term time. He takes this commitment seriously in order to find out more about the beneficiaries of the scholarship. Scholars are expected to return to their own countries and contribute to national development. The course is administered by the UCL School of Public Policy and takes place in the Rubin Building. A lunch meeting was organised, and I attended with the School Director and my course tutor. I was amazed by Mr Rubin's modesty and genuine interest in my aspirations and future. I fear I was billionaire-struck and didn't respond well to his questions, but at the end of our meeting he handed me his card and promised to support me through his networks. A week after our meeting he did indeed make several introductions to influential people in London who all proved invaluable.

The EMPA requires a capstone project instead of a traditional dissertation. Capstones can be undertaken with an existing organisation or as independent research on a policy-related topic of choice. I wanted to work with a governance institution that focused on African public policy; the Mo Ibrahim Foundation came to mind. To the amusement of one of my professors, I decided that I wanted to influence policies that would promote the increase of female presidents by 25% in the African Union by 2030. Another professor liked the idea, but thought it was unrealistic and overambitious. I disagreed, saying that not attempting to stimulate the policy dialogue was more of an issue and simply a way of accepting the status quo. It was a poignant moment for me; President Ellen Johnson Sirleaf of Liberia was stepping down after successfully and peacefully serving her tenure. She was the first female head of state in the African Union. I found her departure with no other female presidents on the horizon both of great interest and disturbing. Finally I was able to convince my supervisors and my capstone project was entitled 'Women's Absence from Presidential Leadership in the African Union and Implications for the African Union Agenda 2063'.

Once agreed, I checked the Mo Ibrahim Foundation (MIF) website to find out more about their work and the possibility of undertaking my capstone project with them. To my surprise and delight, I found out that Baroness Amos, was a board member and I decided to contact her. Even though I hadn't seen her much since our first memorable meeting which had sparked my return to Sierra Leone, I was an avid follower. In February 2016, when she was Director at the School of African and Oriental Studies (SOAS) I had had the opportunity of paying her a personal visit to update her on my progress since 2007, and she had encouraged me to stay in touch.

Myself and President Ellen Johnson Sirleaf

After accepting the Pentland Scholarship in May 2017 I had notified Valerie, and she had sent me a congratulatory message. It was therefore easier for me to reconnect with her regarding an introduction to MIF to discuss my project. Nonetheless, I was nervous when I contacted her, but she responded the same day asking for a synopsis of the project and for my request to be forwarded to MIF. Although I was delighted, I was also panic-stricken. I didn't want to let her down, which might mean rejection. I worked hard to send her the best version of what I believed was a convincing two-page document. A few days later, she sent me an email requesting me to attend a meeting with the Executive Director of MIF, Nathalie Delapalme.

I couldn't believe my luck that this was happening. I met Madame Delapalme at her office in central London in March 2018 and she was intrigued by my project. I said I would like to interview the two elected female presidents in the African Union: Ellen Johnson Sirleaf of Liberia and Joyce Banda of Malawi. To my great surprise, she told me that Ellen Johnson Sirleaf was the recipient of the 2017 Mo Ibrahim Prize. It was awarded to African presidents who met the strict criteria of good governance during their tenure. She would be receiving the award in Kigali, Rwanda, in April 2018 during the Mo Ibrahim Governance weekend. Madame Delapalme offered to introduce me to her personal assistant to arrange a meeting for me to interview President Johnson Sirleaf. President Banda wouldn't be attending, but there would be women leaders at a special women's meeting during the three-day programme. I was also officially invited to attend the event in Kigali. I was totally overwhelmed by the outcome of this meeting; it felt totally unreal.

As we were leaving, I noticed a man who looked like Dr Mo Ibrahim. Madame Delapalme asked whether I wanted to say hello. Apparently, he wasn't normally in the office, but he had come in to see them. Mo Ibrahim was enthusiastic and well informed about Sierra Leone. I spent about five minutes with him and he encouraged me to continue with my work. A great believer in gender equality, he joked that the Foundation was beginning to look unequal because there were more women. I took a picture of us and left full of excitement. I couldn't wait to share the news with my professors. I felt like I was in a film.

Madame Delapalme put me in touch with President Sirleaf's office and my interview with her was confirmed for the morning of the award ceremony, 27 April 2018. I had the required consent form approved by Professor Weale in readiness and my supervisors were pleasantly surprised and excited about my progress, supporting me throughout the entire process.

The exclusive interview with Ellen Johnson Sirleaf took place at the Marriot Hotel in Kigali. I asked my friend and mentee, Fatou to accompany me to take notes, but it was unnecessary as Johnson Sirleaf kindly allowed us to record it. Fatou and I are confident Sierra Leonean women who believe nothing will faze us. However, we felt overwhelmed in the presence of this powerful woman. She had shattered the glass ceiling by becoming the first democratically elected female president in Africa and successfully completed two terms. I had met President Sirleaf a few times when I was Gender Adviser to the President of Sierra Leone, including being assigned to her during the inauguration ceremony for the second term of our president. But I had never had the opportunity to talk to her. Now, here we were, just the three of us.

The interview focused on her journey to the presidency and her time in office. President Sirleaf spoke candidly about her experiences, including the challenges she faced during her tenure. She started by telling me that as a young girl she never told people she wanted to become president, but growing up she voiced her opinions and took positions. In her professional life she stood for certain things and expressed them freely. Her mother was a teacher, a preacher and a courageous woman whose attributes were inherited by her children. Madam Johnson Sirleaf told me she believed in hard work, and that got her the presidency:

> 'I ascended step by step until I became a Minister. I represented my country, along with other officials of government, and in those meetings, I stood out because I was factual, I was courageous to take [an] independent stance…even if it was unpopular. And I have been a strong activist. So, every rung on the ladder gave you more stamina, more determination and I think, one needs to have confidence in themselves. That self confidence that tells you, "I can make it. I can be what I want to be." I am willing to pursue my goals to overcome all the obstacles and distractions that you are bound to face on the road to success.'

This was a very powerful moment for both Fatou and me. It was valuable, real mentorship at the highest level that we had not expected. But I was also interested in her successes and asked President Johnson Sirleaf to tell me about her legacy as the first female

Executive President of Liberia and Africa. She smiled proudly and said:

'I think the first overwhelming part of my legacy is Sustained Peace. Our country had been at war for two decades. The fact that we can today boast of fifteen consecutive years of sustained peace is an experience our country has not known for a while. The young kids today can be proud that they do not know a gun and they do not have to run. So peace is the overwhelming legacy.

Freedom, I think I gave my country a voice, particularly women. Rural women today can stand up and say: "Madam President, because of you I can now participate in meetings because we were excluded before."'

She further stated that women's participation increased during her tenure and Liberia now has women Chiefs because of freedom. Madam Johnson Sirleaf also spoke about the freedom of civil society organisations and giggled about taking a lot of political beatings from the media because she allowed freedom of expression and protected the freedom of the people. As a female president she said:

'I think what I brought in as a woman was the part about compromise, the adjustment, inclusiveness that enabled us to have that peace and enabled us to protect that freedom.'

President Johnson Sirleaf spoke candidly about male dominance and the Ebola Virus as two key challenges during her administration. She told me that, although she was a woman president and could generate women's participation and empowerment, it was very complicated because the administration was predominately male. On the issue of the Gender Equality Bill, Madam Johnson Sirleaf said:

'Some of the things I wanted, like the Equity Bill to bring more women into Parliament through constitutional change, policy change and legal change, weren't achieved. I wish we could have had more women ... in our cabinet.'

She stated that the years of women not having access to full participation and equality had limited the chances of more representation because they were not prepared. She spoke about the political manoeuvres she had to overcome and how complicated it was to achieve her goals.

On Ebola, President Johnson Sirleaf spoke about the devasting impact on the economy:

'First of all, it destroyed our economy because growth plummeted to zero. Growth rate that

had [*sic*] has been climbing to 9% came down
to zero because investors left the country.'

I could feel the sadness in her voice as she described
the destruction Ebola had caused and the impact
it had had. She said that this was the most difficult
challenge but was happy that they did not accept
the predications and they challenged the situation.
Madam Johnson Sirleaf spoke about how she went to
work, bringing together her people, and encouraged
the medical personnel, especially as they were also
dying. She went out, took the risk to be with them,
and proudly concluded that her country was able to
defeat Ebola.

At the end of the interview, I wanted President Johnson Sirleaf to advise the next generation of women
leaders on what was needed to uphold her legacy and
get more women presidents in the African Union. In a
very subtle and motherly manner she said:

'I think we have to encourage networking.
We have to continue the debate, bring different groups together for a discussion on the
experiences of women. Identifying the models
that are out there, and there are many in different areas, women standing out and bringing all that together. Bring women and young
girls together to discuss those experiences to
identify where the obstacles are, also where

the constraints remain and how we go about addressing them.'

I, and many more women and girls in Africa, would embark on implementing this valuable advice from President Ellen Johnson Sirleaf. She has no intention of retiring from activism and hopes to continue being part of the movement. As a commitment to the cause, on 8 March 2020 she established the Ellen Johnson Sirleaf Presidential Center for Women and Development to advance women's public leadership. I look forward to visiting the centre in future.

Later in the day, I attended the women's meeting, a side event where women from all over the world debated the way forward in promoting women's political empowerment within the African Union. It was essentially a discussion of the topic of my capstone project. Women leaders spoke of their frustration at not having another female head of state in the AU after President Johnson Sirleaf. Mrs Mary Robinson, the former President of the Republic of Ireland, was at the table next to me. I had officially met Mrs Robinson at an energy conference in Vienna in 2013 and when she had visited Sierra Leone as UN Human Rights Commissioner, but I had never had the chance to speak to her personally. I seized the opportunity to talk to her during a short break and requested an interview for my capstone project. To my surprise, she was very interested and granted me an interview the following morning. Although she wasn't an African

woman or executive president, I wanted to understand the dynamics of her time in office as a woman.

When I arrived for the interview, her husband was
present; she wanted him to stay. I was quite happy
because I was also interested in his perspective as the
husband of a female president. One of the key things I
learned was that Mrs Robinson had proffered support
to both President Joyce Banda and President Johnson
Sirleaf. She also confirmed what President Johnson
Sirleaf had said about being lonely at the top and how
it was important for women to support each other
at that level, regardless of what continent they were
on. Mr Robinson also described how people used to
address him as 'President' and that he had to remind
them that he was actually the president's spouse.
These revelations were significant for my research. We
ended the interview with photographs and Mrs Robinson told me to stay in touch and keep her updated on
my progress, especially in political decision-making.

What I learned from meeting these powerful and
influential people is that you should never doubt your
instincts in the pursuit of what you want. Staying in
touch, regardless of whether you receive feedback or
not, is a powerful tool. My persistence in keeping in
contact with Baroness Amos following a chance social
meeting afforded me a whole new world of possibilities. It opened the door to many more influential
people. It also entailed sacrificing my limited financial
resources to purchase flights to Rwanda, whatever the
cost. But during that trip I met lots of people, includ-

ing a BBC journalist who was moderating some of the main events. Later in the year she reached out and invited me to an interview on the BBC Focus on Africa television programme to speak about women in politics in Africa. That interview had a substantial audience and was shared widely on different platforms, including the MIF social media sites.

In September 2018 I graduated with a Masters in Public Administration, specialising in Global Public Policy and Management, from the Robert F Wagner Graduate School of Public Service, NYU and School of Public Policy, UCL.

5
Giving Back

Time to return home

Almost eighteen months after my memorable meeting with Baroness Amos, I decided to implement her advice and returned home in 2009. Life in London was becoming difficult after the financial crisis of 2008. Although I had a job, my social life was suffering because many of my friends were affected by the crisis. I was also tired of living on my own and I missed my daughter. The perfect opportunity to say goodbye to London came when the QCA announced that they would be moving to Coventry and my well-paid consultancy would automatically end. Friends were shocked when I told them about my relocation plans to Sierra Leone. No one expected it because both my professional and private lives seemed perfect. Yes,

I would miss London, but I decided to go back. However, returning to Sierra Leone in 2009 had its own challenges.

I returned home with no political influence or promise of getting a job. I went home with an open mind to explore different opportunities, especially in business. Although the country was still recovering from a horrific Civil War, there had already been two successful presidential elections, including one in 2007. A new government was in power and the President had undertaken a robust campaign to encourage people from the diaspora to return home. I joined hundreds of Sierra Leoneans returning home to contribute to the post-war reconstruction of their country. Accommodation was challenging because my parents didn't own a home. I initially stayed with my dearest Uncle Dauda who was a minister in the government. He has always been a strong male influence in my life and has watched me grow up.

I was totally clueless about politics, with no interest in working for the government. I preferred being an entrepreneur and decided to expand my hair business from London to Freetown – especially after a bad beauty treatment experience in Freetown during my last visit. I soon realised that there were no decent salons catering for the returning diaspora and diplomatic communities. Owning a salon promised to be a good business opportunity, but the challenges included a lack of staff who were qualified and trained in hairdressing and product knowledge. I had very grand ideas; I wanted to bring Mayfair to Freetown. But I needed all the right ingredients for it to work out, including the right location and space. My goal was to establish a Jemna Hair Studio franchise similar to the big salon brands in London. Getting it right from the outset was crucial. I embarked on finding a location and sourcing hair products.

Electricity was a luxury in Freetown and generators were the norm. Mosquitos were rampant with high levels of malaria, which I was also a victim of. Thankfully, the new Davidson Nicol hospital was well equipped with qualified doctors and nurses who treated me successfully. The social scene was buzzing and the nightlife in Aberdeen, around the beach area, was lively. While I was recovering from malaria, I met a friend at the golf club. He liked what I was trying to do with the salon business and wanted to support me. He later offered me accommodation in one of the hotel suites that his brother owned so that I had somewhere I could stay and commence my business. That singular act of kindness created the security I needed to embark on my new life in Sierra Leone as a returnee.

Jemna Hair Studios

My London business meant that I had already established relationships with product manufacturers and I contacted them to discuss my new business venture.

Although I wanted to continue with the two product lines I had in London, I quickly found out that I would need to work with African distributors. This was a great opportunity for me to become a distributor and supply other businesses. After contacting Avlon's head office in Chicago, they were delighted to work with me and I was offered the second distributorship in West Africa to exclusively supply their professional hair products: KeraCare, Avlon and Syntonics. In addition, my business could deliver professional training, including international certification, to Sierra Leonean hairdressers. With this great news, I intensified my search for the perfect premises. Fortunately, I found the ideal location and space, although it was extremely expensive at $12,000 per annum.

I signed the rental agreement, started renovations on the property and ordered my shop equipment and furniture from London. I flew to Chicago to meet the Director of Business Development and the owner of Avlon to discuss further elements of our business partnership. This included using my apartment complex, still under construction, to establish a hair and beauty training academy. As a distributor, I needed to place a minimum order of $10,000, which was honoured and the first order was shipped. The company promised to send two senior personnel to train the first cohort of my staff and those in the salons that would be stocking the products. My salon was going to be designed as a training hub and distribution centre. I was very excited about this development and returned to Freetown to set up the salon.

I had invested heavily in the business from the sale of my main UK home and my hopes were extremely high. We discussed plans to establish the Jemna franchise all over the country and within the Mano River Union. I wanted to buy a generator, but my business neighbour offered the shared use of their 17 KVA generator. I would only need to buy fuel. They also helped me clear my goods from customs, which used to be a difficult and complicated process. While waiting for my shipments, I embarked on a three-month intensive customer service training programme for the staff. Bad customer service was the norm in Sierra Leone and I wanted my business to set a precedent of high-level customer care and prove how it positively affects business growth. I trained my staff to take pride in their work and instilled a culture of respect, integrity and loyalty. Personal grooming was a key part of the business, and I encouraged them to take ownership of this because its success relied on our collective responsibility. They were trained not to tolerate any form of abuse from clients and clear reporting guidelines were established. My initial intake comprised young women and men in their early twenties, ranging from no formal education to secondary school certificates. What was inspiring about them was their readiness to learn. They were excited and proud to be part of this new establishment. The success of my business depended on these young people and I wanted them to know and feel that I valued them above anything else. It worked.

I had the right location, staff and products, and the best clientele. We had a beautiful space upstairs for a café serving tea, coffee and wine. Jemna was the place to be and I was truly excited. My hair extension partners in Los Angeles came on board and the finest weaves in the world were sold at Jemna. Business was thriving. Within a few months the senior Avlon executives arrived to train my staff, plus the owners of fifteen other salons. We wanted salon owners to know that we weren't in competition with them and wanted to provide a support system to enhance their growth. Unfortunately, many of the salons didn't have the funds to buy the products and asked for them on a credit basis. This was a risk I wasn't prepared to take. I was also worried about protecting the brands; it would be easy for people to mix or dilute the products in order to save money. Safeguarding my product lines was a priority. For me to stock a salon, they had to prove their integrity and that I could trust them. The clientele at Jemna was diverse, but it was mostly people like me who had returned to Sierra Leone, the international community and the local middle classes. We had cocktail networking evenings with live bands hosted by local celebrities. These were very popular with many of our clients.

United for Humanity

Returning to Sierra Leone and giving back to my country involved different aspects. Although we are considered a hospitable society, giving back on an international level wasn't one of our strengths. Aid dependency had created a culture of taking; I wanted to influence a cognitive shift by promoting a culture of giving back. Many people, including my brother-in-law, had sacrificed their lives during the bloody Civil War to bring us peace. I thought we should reach out to other nations, not just through our government, but through local organisations. I decided to connect with a few friends to raise funds to support victims of the Haiti earthquake in 2010. I felt we should not rely on the excuse of poverty for not helping others internationally. The government had already donated $100,000 and Sierra Leoneans were complaining that our country didn't have enough money to give to others. We wanted to change these feelings and promote a spirit of giving and volunteering. Along with about eight other people from different professional backgrounds and the entertainment industry, we formed United for Humanity to organise a benefit concert for Haiti. We quickly learned that we needed to formalise the group in order to raise funds and be able to send them abroad. The organisation was formally registered by a renowned female lawyer, Mrs Sally Khtumal, who undertook this task pro bono. Women like her made my return to Sierra Leone worthwhile.

The concert raised approximately $12,000 from ticket sales and donations. Africell was extremely helpful with their support, including a PA system, banners and their Communications Manager working with us the entire evening. A businessman who owned one of the prestigious hotels on the beach provided the venue. All celebrities, including an internationally renowned female icon, donated their time. The United Nations Peacebuilding Office in Sierra Leone (UNIPSIL) also partnered with us, and the Executive Representative of the UN Secretary-General (ERSG) was our guest of honour. The event was well received, and we successfully transferred $10,400 to Haiti for the permanent resettlement of four families through an organisation called One Dome at a Time. The UN was impressed with our achievement and I found myself headhunted to join their organisation.

Back to business

The business climate in Sierra Leone was not conducive to start-ups. The challenges were enormous and small- and medium-sized businesses were vulnerable to failing because of the high government taxes that appeared to be designed to kill rather than promote business growth. For example, rentals were pegged to the US dollar rate, and access to finance was (and still is) a route to bankruptcy with bank rates starting from 25% APR. It was worse for women: bank staff, including managers, would often sexually exploit women who tried to access finance. The government seemed to want to punish any successful small businesses. A few months after I had opened, the National Revenue Authority came to assess my business in order to determine the business rates and taxes. The officer concluded that I should be paying a higher rate because the place 'looked really nice'. His cosmetic valuation of the business was a killer, designed to instantly send the business into administration before it could even start recording profits.

Another problem involved the companies that supplied electricity and water. Both employed similar modes of harassment which meant that I had to use similar tactics to stop them from interfering in the smooth running of the business. One morning two rather drunk officers from the electricity company demanded payment of bills I had never received and threatened to disconnect us if I didn't pay straightaway. I told them I hadn't received any bills and the limited electricity supply meant we were incurring huge fuel costs to run the generator. Apparently it was my responsibility to collect my bills from the electricity company. In the end I had to ask two young employees, who also acted as our security guards, to physically remove them from the premises and make sure they didn't disconnect us outside the building. At least this stopped them from harassing my business. I had to do the same with the water company. But this time I used very strong language, which shocked the men, and I drove to their office threatening to call a press conference to expose the water company's exploitative methods.

Despite these challenges, business was thriving, customer retention was high, and the time invested in the staff training was reflected in our revenue. Hair products were flying off the shelves, and the café became very popular for tea, wine and light snacks. As I needed to buy more products and I had exhausted my personal funds, I decided to take out a loan. At the time, I didn't consider the interest rate as being much of an issue; the Managing Director of the bank was forward-looking and encouraged me to take out the loan. I used my unfinished property as collateral because I could see the opportunity for growth, including the franchise of Jemna. Once the loan was approved, I ordered my goods through the bank.

What immediately became evident when I was trying to access finance for my business was the accepted norm of sexual harassment. Bank officials at all levels routinely used subtle or blatant sexual advances with female-led businesses by taking advantage of unsustainable high-interest (25–28%) loans, plus the threat of losing their business and collateral if the business didn't perform well. I was not immune to this practice, nor was one of my staff members. One senior bank official was pleasant and supportive of my business until I tried to access finance from his bank. Suddenly, I became the most beautiful woman in his eyes, and he tried to seduce me with lines of credit for anything I wanted. What he didn't know was that I knew about his reputation and I was prepared for his advances. I turned him down, but I was one of the lucky ones.

Who knows what would have happened if it was my last resort: many women have no alternative.

Another bank executive tried to rape one of my female staff when she went to his house for his weekly grooming routine, including manicure, pedicure and massage. Apparently, he had already been sexually harassing her, but she was afraid to tell me. She thought I might not believe her and wanted to handle the situation herself. She was an independent contractor and a single parent; she needed every penny she could earn. But things became intolerable when he locked the door and tried to rape her and then masturbated in front of her. She came to me to complain about him, looking visibly upset. I immediately phoned the man and threatened to expose him for his behaviour. The woman told me that his behaviour was commonplace and if I did take action, it would affect her business. He got away with an apology and I deleted him from our list of clients.

Within a year the business was thriving. Then the government decided to reconstruct Wilkinson Road, the road where our business was located, with practically no prior consultation with affected businesses. I never heard personally from the Ministry of Works nor did my business receive official notification of these major disruptions. My understanding was that they communicated with landlords and not tenants, but the news quickly spread and within two weeks work had started. The frequent loss of electricity meant we had

LEAVE IT TO NAASU

huge fuel costs for the generator. I watched as they got closer to my business and I saw my investment literally disappearing before my eyes. The dust was unbearable and parking for our customers, which had been a huge selling point, became virtually impossible. My fuel costs tripled because I needed to keep the products cool. In order to save money, I moved 80% of the stock to my house. As it was becoming financially difficult to sustain the business, I applied for a job at the UN to supplement my earnings and help with the running costs. We experienced sporadic drops in sales, and staff were demoralised because they thought the business was going to close. A large quantity of products got damaged, which we were unable to sell. I fell back on loan repayments because not even my UN salary could save the situation. They were desperate and difficult times and I had gambled funds I could have used to pay for my daughter's university fees. I was feeling despondent about the way things had turned out.

I rented out my office to one of my customers when I started my job at the UN. By all accounts she was trustworthy. The money provided some relief and allowed me to pay some outstanding bills, including the rent of my hairdressing business. My worst nightmare came true when I got a call from my manager while I was away on assignment to tell me that my neighbour wanted to stop sharing the generator. The complete lack of consideration and indifference as to how it would impact my business was shocking. I immediately lost trust in people. My lowest point was when I heard that the generator was removed while some customers were still under dryers and others in the middle of their treatments. It was an awful moment.

I returned to Freetown to look for a replacement generator, but they were too expensive and I couldn't afford one. Someone told me I could buy one on hire purchase, but all my efforts turned out to be futile. I asked my office tenant whether she could let us use one of the generators from her home temporarily, but that didn't materialise either. I decided to look for a smaller place to rescue the remaining stock. Eventually I found out that my tenant had been secretly conspiring with the landlord to take over the entire premises. That's why she had refused to bring her generator to help rescue my business. She was also trying to lure my staff away by offering them more money. In the end they told me everything: one of them had accepted her offer. I eventually found an unfurnished place 80% smaller than my previous premises for half the price. My options were limited: I either had to accept or close the business totally. The business moved to the new location, which meant my former tenant could immediately move into my former premises and install a generator.

Once my anger had subsided, I realised I would need to look to myself for the solution. I knew the buck stopped with me and I had to make serious decisions going forward. I had the painful task of telling staff that I had to reduce numbers. They had the option to stay or leave. Fortunately, those that I really wanted and I felt cared, stayed with me. We were back in business and most of our loyal customers followed us. But I had an overbearing landlady who tried to involve herself in my business affairs. When she saw the calibre of my customers, she started making unreasonable demands with little regard to what had been agreed in the contract. She even counted the cars to justify an increase in rent. To my horror, when it started raining a wall became soaked and unusable because of the danger of electrocution. Our small space had reduced by 50% and the landlady had no intention of sorting out the problem. It was obvious that the business was becoming a financial and emotional disaster. My new job with the government also required my fullest attention. Although it was painful, the start of more roadworks meant that after four years of trading, it was time to close down Jemna Hair Studio with an outstanding bank loan. I was personally responsible for the loan and had used my unfinished property as collateral. I needed a fresh start to get myself back on track to make sure I didn't lose my house.

This whole experience taught me some important lessons. You can do all the right things, but circumstances beyond your control can make or break your success. How you interpret the situation determines whether you have lost or won. I felt like I won because I gained both positive and bitter experiences from running a business. There are some fundamental errors that

I would never repeat. These include pouring all my personal funds into a business and being too emotionally involved. Although it's easier said than done, emotions should be detached from entrepreneurship. But the most important lesson was the power of trust and betrayal. I trusted my neighbours and depended on our arrangement, which is why I never thought of buying my own generator. If I hadn't been so comfortable with a verbal agreement my business could have possibly survived. Renting space to a customer was another transaction based on trust, not realising her agenda was to put me out of business. She succeeded and I felt betrayed. However, I emerged a more decisive and stronger woman, which has benefited both my professional and private lives. You own and control your own story and the giving-back experience, both from our fundraising concert and giving back to my country in general, is worth all the other challenges.

6
Power

Exercising your agency

I was encouraged to apply for a position at UNIPSIL following the benefit concert for Haiti. The leadership team knew that I had a postgraduate degree in gender and international development. Initially I declined because I wanted to focus on my business. But as things started changing on the business front, I decided to apply. In 2010 I was appointed to the post of Gender Officer in the Human Rights Section at UNIPSIL. My key role was to engage the Sowies (traditional leaders and circumcisers) on the issue of female circumcision. Female circumcision is an extremely difficult and sensitive topic in Sierra Leone because it is an integral ritual for membership into the powerful and secret women's Bondo Society. Anyone who dared to speak against the practice faced the wrath of the Sowies. The government would not discuss the Bondo Society because this went against all tradition and culture and it would be political suicide. Although I was an initiate of the Bondo Society, I had also written my undergraduate Psychology thesis on understanding the meaning of circumcision within the context of the Bondo Society. The combination of my membership and research background made me an ideal candidate. Although it wasn't obvious to me at first, it made sense why UNIPSIL were so keen on recruiting me.

We agreed on the terms of reference, including not using the expression female genital mutilation (FGM) due to its negative connotations and the possibility of a backlash from stakeholders. I was given the mandate to lead the work on female circumcision with traditional leaders, including Paramount Chiefs and the Bondo Society. This was a hugely sensitive and, to some extent, dangerous task, but I was ready to deliver on it without disrespect or compromising the integrity of all the parties involved. I commenced work after gaining permission and support from my own Sowie and her leadership in Kenema district, Eastern Sierra Leone. This was, and still is, a traditional hotspot for strong views on the Bondo Society. It was therefore a powerful and historic endorsement to have their unqualified support. Leading women and journalists who tried to speak openly against the activities of the Bondo Society faced severe danger, including forced initiations. Without this support, it would have been impossible to for me to perform my role.

In order to understand the dynamics of the Society, I began by inviting the national heads of Sowies to regional workshops to find out their views on collaborating with the UN to empower women and girls with an aim to ending all forms of violence. My tactic was to allow the issue of female circumcision to emerge naturally through the wider discussions. A group of Sowies in Freetown had established themselves as the national body, but I quickly learned that they weren't connected to any members in the provinces. I enlisted their support and asked them to join me in engaging their sisters across the country. The ethos of the Bondo Society is about women's empowerment and I wanted to leverage this crucial aspect to hold this influential institution accountable on all the issues affecting women and girls nationally.

We started in the Northern Province where the Regional Human Rights UN Office invited Sowie leaders from all five districts to a two-day workshop. Approximately one hundred traditional women, including local Chiefs, attended. During the introductions they immediately reprimanded the Western Area Sowies and fined them for referring to themselves as the national body. It was a very interesting and dynamic situation. A symbolic fine was paid, and it was agreed that at the end of the regional meetings a legitimate national body would be formed. Key issues that the women discussed included indifference and stigmatisation by the international community. They felt they were also victims of gender-based violence; their views must be respected to facilitate any discussion on Bondo issues, and their leadership was sacrosanct. In return they would be prepared to work with both the UN and the government to end gender-based violence in Sierra Leone. I told them I was there to collate their views for presentation to the senior leadership at the UN and to hopefully organise a bilateral conference. At the end of the two-day meeting we agreed to establish structures to facilitate constructive dialogue between the UN and the Sowies at district level. The inaugural Sowie Councils were formed from the five northern region districts with temporary Executives.

The same methodology was used to engage a total of 360 Sowies and female Paramount Chiefs in the Eastern, Southern and Western Districts. The conclusions were similar across regions. The most important outcome of this assignment was for Sowies to consider ending child initiation rites of passage, including female circumcision for girls under eighteen. This was a huge breakthrough and an entry point for further discussions on strategies to eliminate violence against women and girls.

I presented the findings of these national Sowie workshops to UNIPSIL and the UN Country Team in Sierra Leone. UN Women decided to support the formation of the Sowie Councils and the United Nations Population Fund (UNFPA) led the formation of Community Advocacy Groups (CAGs) as structures for reducing maternal mortality. Sowies had traditionally acted as birth attendants, as women trusted them to deliver their babies rather than going to hospital. The strategy by UNFPA to convert that role into CAGs immediately showed positive results; Sowies started taking or referring pregnant women to health centres to give birth. Bridging that gap was critical in accelerating progress towards ending maternal and child mortality in Sierra Leone.

Finally, a representative group of the Sowie Councils visited UNIPSIL to thank the leadership for the historic dialogue and to offer their unconditional support in working on the implementation of UN Security Council Resolutions 1325 & 1820 in promoting Women, Peace and Security, which had been the key tenet of the national dialogue workshops. A national conference of traditional female leaders took place in Bo in the Southern Province, with approximately 800 women and representatives from UN Agencies. It was agreed that the female Paramount Chiefs, would lead the implementation of the conclusions between the UN, government, Council of Paramount Chiefs and the Sowies. In order to maintain traditional etiquette, it was proposed that Cultural Centres of Excellence would be established to train girls under eighteen and those women who chose not to be initiated into the Bondo Society. The women agreed that they would work with the government and present their plan on how to end circumcision for underage children.

UNIPSIL, on the other hand, further encouraged and supported the National Sowie Council to use their influence and reach to register first-time female voters for the upcoming 2012 general elections. It was a successful strategy that resulted in the highest numbers of first-time female voters, and I was reliably informed by the UN leadership that it was acknowledged in the UN Secretary-General's Report on Sierra Leone. This ground-breaking work created a productive platform and influenced the discourse on female circumcision in Sierra Leone. The ownership of the process by traditional leaders and trust in my message were critical factors in the success of this initiative. Although engaging the Sowies was one of my key roles, I was also involved in some of the internal decisions in the UN, including the biggest pay reforms for local staff with back payments up to six months and a 30% increase in salaries.

Although I had done well, my supervisor was not happy with some of the strategies I employed with the Sowies. She started to create obstacles for me. A few other women I came into contact with at the UN were also not keen on my presence. I later understood that they hadn't expected the role of the Gender Officer to be so powerful. But I worked hard and produced impactful results within a very short time; senior people were listening to me. As the relationship with my boss deteriorated, I was reassigned as Gender Adviser to the Head of Mission, which caused some anger in the organisation. Rumours were spread to attack me personally and undermine my work with my new boss.

In 2011, during this period of turmoil, there was a Cabinet reshuffle and the Minister of Social Welfare, Gender and Children's Affairs was sacked. I wrote privately to the President describing the attitudes and problems involved in the gender ministry. I emphasised that gender was a serious developmental issue and hoped he could appoint ministers who were technically qualified to lead on it. The ministry was also under resourced with one of the lowest budgetary allocations. I had first met the President during a helicopter ride when I accompanied the UN Women country representative to Magbruka for International Women's Day. I had sat opposite him and felt rather intimidated by his presence. However, this chance meeting gave me the confidence to take a risk and write directly to him. As I wasn't sure whether the letter would reach him, I omitted my contact details.

I was totally oblivious to the political undertones between the presidential State House and the UN Head of Mission. Unless you were directly involved in political affairs, you wouldn't have been aware of these sensitive issues. I later realised that I had innocently entered into a serious diplomatic war between the government and UN.

A few days after sending the letter, I received a phone call from the State Chief of Protocol who was rather irritated with me because the President had read the letter but there was no contact number. I apologised and told him it was just some harmless professional advice from a citizen and I hadn't expected a reply. He told me he would get back to me if necessary. A couple of months later, a colleague from the office called me to say the Chief of Staff (COS) at State House was trying to contact me and could he pass on my number. I was rather alarmed and asked my friend if he knew what it was about. He said no but I should soon find out. Moments later I received a call from the COS requesting that I meet him at State House that afternoon. I told him that I couldn't attend during working hours unless it was official and approved by the Head of Mission. He assured me that protocol would be followed if necessary, but first he needed to meet me. I had no idea what it was all about and I agreed to meet him after work.

He told me that the President had asked him to request a secondment for me from the UN to join the team that was organising the Sierra Leone Conference on Development and Transformation (SLCDT) as a technical adviser on gender. He wanted to know whether I was interested before making a formal request. He also asked whether I was a member of a political party, which I wasn't. At the end of the meeting, I gave my permission for the three-month secondment to be officially requested from the UN. The COS told me that they would cover my salary during this period, once it was agreed. I was both relieved and happy to be considered for such an opportunity to serve my country. However, I had no idea that daggers were drawn, and I had just become a pawn in a rather messy divorce battle. On the other hand, there were some serious internal issues going on and I looked forward to this temporary escape. I was never notified that the request had been sent, nor did Human Resources know about it, as it was sent directly to the Head of Mission. I was furious when I found out that he had responded in a one-line letter rejecting the request.

I found the situation extremely disheartening as I was already involved in a dispute at work. When I commenced my assignment with the UN, I wanted to do so as a British citizen. This was refused and I was told that I couldn't be a diplomat in my own country, even though there were precedents. I was forced to accept a position as a national, earning approximately $5,000 less. Therefore I decided to make the request from the President to serve my country a personal battle. I followed all the protocols to have the official secondment request on my file. Unfortunately, the letter had been destroyed. I made a formal complaint to the UN Secretariat and resigned on principle. I then accepted the three-month post as technical adviser on gender. I subsequently found out that there was a serious problem between the Head of Mission and the government, and he was later asked to leave the country. I never spoke about my situation with anyone from the government as it was under UN investigation and we were forbidden to discuss it. I had to suffer a smear campaign over something I wasn't privy to before I left the UN. I am not sure whether knowing would have influenced my decision to take on the government role, but I probably would have arrived at the same conclusion as a matter of principle. The preliminary finding of my complaint to the UN concluded when both of us had left the UN system. I was satisfied with the ruling and didn't pursue any further action.

Politics/Government

In November 2011, I started working with the government as Gender Specialist with the Secretariat of the SLCDT, reporting to the national co-ordinator. The conference was supervised by the Office of the Chief of Staff. I didn't know what to expect in this new environment, but I had to learn very quickly. On my first day, I was shown my office and introduced to other members of the team. The co-ordinator arranged for his car to pick me up for work since I didn't have an official car. It appeared very organised and unlike what I had expected. On my second day, I found two men occupying 'my office'. I greeted them politely and asked them why they were there. Apparently it was their office, and no one had informed them that it had been reassigned. I reached out to the co-ordinator, who apologised and told me that another office was under renovation and I would move within a week. Considering that this was a three-month contract, the last thing I needed was not having a permanent office. What I didn't realise was that this was a deliberate ploy to set me up for failure because of being directly brought in by the President. From the outside, this would seem like something positive, but I had just been dropped into the jungle of partisan politics where no mercy was shown to unknown entities who attracted the President's attention. It was my baptism of fire into the world of dirty politics. However, my inexperience was an advantage because I kept to the rules and documented any issues. This was not the norm in government where you flaunt rules and get protection from 'political parents'.

Nearly a month into my tenure, nothing much was happening apart from accompanying the co-ordinator to meetings as though I were a secretary. Then he was away travelling, leaving my situation unresolved; but I still had the use of his vehicle. On the surface, it may have appeared that I was second-in-command, but behind the scenes, every effort for me to fail was being orchestrated. My request to engage women in the provinces was turned down, even after I contributed to help facilitate a substantial fund of nearly half a million dollars. I couldn't understand why it was happening. Gradually I became friends with the two men who had occupied my office on that second day, and everything became clear. They had decided to support me and my work and helped turned things around; they felt they should do it for the good of the country. My role was gradually downgraded because people needed to access the funds; I became more and more frustrated as I was deliberately made to feel incompetent. Other women were sent to help me without my asking; another ploy to undermine me. The showdown came at what should have been the final steering committee meeting, chaired by the President.

Almost all of those present assured the President that we were ready to host the SLCDT. I listened in amazement to these blatant lies. I had only managed to engage one group of women and had not been allowed to undertake any district or regional meetings to collate women's perspectives. Yet here we were with people boldly stating that the conference should proceed. I was fuming. Finally, it was time for questions and contributions. Towards the end, the President asked me to speak. I could see the tension in the faces of some of my colleagues and their hostile expressions. I calmly objected to holding the conference in December and explained to the committee that I had not been given the opportunity to execute my duties and therefore had been unable to gather the regional perspectives from women. It was my opinion that the conference could not be held without the important voices of the women of Sierra Leone. My conclusion was direct: women were not ready to hold this consultation. I moved a motion on behalf of women and asked the President to postpone the conference until their voices were incorporated. At the end of the meeting he thanked the committee for their hard work and re-emphasised his promise to hold a consultative conference. However, he agreed with me and stated that he had no intention of upsetting the women of his country. For that reason, the conference would be postponed for a month to ensure women's perspectives were fully incorporated. I was pleased, but there were many upset faces in the room. On the other hand, I had my two office friends firmly on my side. The following morning I appeared standing next to the President on almost every media outlet. It was an early Christmas present for me and I decided to go to London to join my daughter for the holidays.

While I was in London, I almost resigned because of the continued attempts to undermine my job. In my absence they had formed a committee of women and allocated them funds which they had refused to disburse to me to implement my terms of reference. I reached out to a woman I respected, and she advised me to return and to stand up to them and take ownership of my role. I took her advice and returned more determined than ever to succeed. A women's conference and vigil had already been planned and funded. I attended both and once I explained to the women how I had been treated, they threw their support behind me. They had been told that I had asked for additional support because the task was too demanding for me. They didn't realise that they were being used to discredit me. The plot had backfired, and I took charge of the entire process. I also disrupted any plans to take opportunities away from local women in favour of foreign nationals whose husbands were expatriates. I was determined to get things done as stipulated in my terms of reference.

I insisted that all contracts be reassigned to Sierra Leonean women. Although I was unable to get all the money back because some payments had already been disbursed, 70% was returned. The three-day conference finally took place and I was given a small role as master of ceremonies on the first day. This included a wonderful display of women dancing to traditional music composed by one of Sierra Leone's iconic female artists. The performance didn't just captivate the audience; the President publicly instructed the State House cameraman to archive the footage. My official role was given to a woman who was not initially a member of the conference secretariat but used her political influence to take centre stage. In the end, I was pleased to have delivered on my assignment and I left with my professional integrity intact. The final document from the conference would constitute the national strategic blueprint for Sierra Leone's national development plan for the next fifty years.

7
Leadership

The rocky road to State House

I concluded my three-month assignment with the SLCDT; my uncompromising attitude had ruffled senior officials within State House. Although there were rumours that the President wanted me to continue working, there was no official notice to that effect. And based on my recent experience at the SLCDT, I had little interest in working for the government because of the poor ethical standards I had experienced at the very top. Nonetheless, I kept an open mind. I began job hunting and within two months I had two offers from the African Development Bank (ADfB) and the United States Agency for International Development (USAID).

In April 2012, I was at the agricultural show in Kenema organised by the Ministry of Agriculture and attended by the President. During the event, I asked the President's Aide de Camp (ADC) whether it would be possible to meet his boss. He told me that my name could be added to the list of people wanting to meet him, but he couldn't guarantee it. Based on this, I decided to cancel my return trip and wait at the Presidential Lodge. After lunch the President retired for his afternoon break and we were told to return in the evening. They often used this strategy to get rid of people – at least those who did not have direct access to his inner circle. I had already checked out of my hotel and asked whether I could stay within the compound. A close aide was kind enough to let me use one of the rooms for a couple of hours. It meant I was also able to rest and freshen up before returning to the waiting room to add my name to the list. I was number two on the list and it was up to the President whether he would see me. I waited nervously for his decision.

Fortunately, my name was approved. I needed to make good use of this exclusive opportunity to speak directly to the President. During our 15-minute meeting, I questioned him on his commitment towards the empowerment of women and girls. I wanted to know why the Ministry of Gender was treated as a second-class ministry with one of the smallest budgetary allocations. He told me that his belief in women's empowerment was influenced by his mother, two sisters and his two daughters. I further probed whether there was someone in his office who updated him on any upcoming issues that required his attention in promoting gender equality and the empowerment of women. There wasn't anyone, but he would take a special interest in this area and work with the Minister of Gender to instigate improvements. The President had a gift of making one feel at ease to speak freely with him. His body language was welcoming, and he had a ready smile. He also asked what I was doing; I told him that I had been job hunting and just received two offers that I was considering. Just before we finished he asked me to call his ADC whom he instructed to arrange an appointment for me to see him the following week, regardless of his schedule. I had no idea why the President would want to see me; I hadn't asked him for anything personal or a job. I already had my two job offers from USAID and ADfB. Nevertheless, I felt honoured.

On my return, I went to visit the Minister of Gender as I had been helping out on a pro bono basis and the Deputy had been trying to see whether she could get a development partner to pay for this work. I informed the minister about my recent meeting with the President, which he was pleased about. The President was scheduled to inaugurate the opening of two squash courts and he offered me one of the invitations to St Edward's Secondary School. I was stunned at how things were turning out, but I didn't make anything of it. At the end of the inauguration ceremony the President came up to me to ask whether a Senior Executive from his office had contacted me. When he saw that I was struggling to answer, he asked me to call the individual and let him know that the President had just seen me. After multiple panic attacks, I did text him and I received a call from the Confidential Secretary inviting me to State House for a meeting the next day at 7.30am. This would be the first meeting between us since the SLCDT and I knew it wasn't going to be an easy ride.

I arrived at 7.15am and had to wait for nearly three hours. That meeting was one of the most humiliating experiences of my life. I was asked about the details of my meeting with the President and I briefly stated some of the key points. From that point on I was talked down to and belittled. I was informed in no uncertain terms that I shouldn't feel too excited about working at State House because I would be given 'a small desk somewhere to wait for little jobs the President might want me to do'. I should also understand that there were many clever people in the presidency and it would be best if I just sat quietly in a corner. At the end of the meeting I was formally told that the President wanted me to work with him at State House. I would be appointed as a Gender Specialist rather than as an Adviser, even though I would be receiving the same pay and benefits. Despite these blatant bullying tactics, I agreed to everything to facilitate my appointment. This experience gave me the strength to stand up to the system of impunity that was widespread in government. The real battle had started for me, but I remained calm and showed no sign of distress.

A few weeks later I was still waiting for my official appointment and I lobbied to receive an invitation to the Independence celebrations. My plan was to attract the attention of the President, which fortunately I did in the presence of the Senior Executive who had been so belittling. The President asked him about the progress on my appointment as he hadn't seen an appointment letter for his approval. I nearly fainted. The following week, I was asked to collect my appointment letter so that I could commence work on 1 June 2012.

Gender Specialist – Office of the Chief of Staff (OCOS)

Prior to starting work, I had a call from a young lady warning me that plans were afoot not to give me an office in State House. She told me not to accept any suggestions to work elsewhere as it was a plot to undermine my position. Although I was surprised, it wasn't totally unexpected given my past experience. My direct appointment by the President had ruffled feathers and some senior figures were bent on disrupting my appointment and were plotting my downfall. However, I decided to commence duty with an open mind in the hope that things would improve.

I spent my first day sitting in the office meeting room. Nobody said a word to me and this routine continued for a week. Sometimes, I would go into the secretary's office if a meeting was taking place. I was told there was no office provision for my role and I would need to solicit funds from development partners. I sweetly accepted their suggestion and came up with a plan that would strengthen rather than weaken my position. I asked them to write an official letter of introduction explaining my remit to all the development partners, Ministries, Departments and Agencies. Without doubt, that letter, written and signed by the Chief of Staff, was the most important letter of my tenure. I followed it up with requests for courtesy calls and funds to mobilise an office. Soon after receiving the letter, a high-level delegation led by the US Ambassador and Director for West Africa paid a courtesy call at State House to congratulate me and offer their unwavering support. This was followed by other high-level delegations such as Women in Security Sector led by the most high-ranking female officials. This included the only female Brigadier in the Army, female Assistant Inspector General of the Police and a Director of Prisons. There was even an elaborate national event organised by female traditional leaders celebrating my appointment and thanking the President. Over two thousand traditional female leaders, including 90% of the female Paramount Chiefs and leaders, descended on Kenema for the occasion. They had organised it themselves with no financial support from me. The President told the then Minister of Foreign Affairs that he had never seen such an outpouring of gratitude for any appointment, not even for ministers. The level of solidarity and support from the diplomatic community and national institutions was unprecedented. Although some people in State House were unhappy with my appointment, the President saw positive reactions on a national level from all walks of life.

Although I didn't succeed in getting my salary paid by a development partner, two organisations proffered technical and office equipment support. The government later decided to pay all salaries from central funds after a representative of one of the UN Agencies demanded to see the Presidential Advisory Notes as a condition for support. As my appointment gained momentum, I was still told that there was no office space available at State House and the Minister of Gender had been tasked to find me an office. I pretended to be unaware of their plans to keep me out of State House and went along with the various office viewings. After two of these viewings I told the minister what was happening. He immediately stopped looking for an office saying that it made no sense for him to have a senior official from State House within his ministry who wasn't reporting to him.

Having failed to remove me from State House, the Senior Executive summoned me to a meeting. He asked me to find an office outside of State House to which he would personally contribute $12,000 a year towards costs. When I rejected his proposal, it led to a verbal threat of being isolated by the rest of the office and having to work on my own. True to his word, I was given no office supplies and had limited access to transport. While all senior staff had offices, I was asked to share with four analysts. This turned out to be one of the 'best wrongs' they meted out to me. I succeeded in my role principally from gaining an insider's perspective from these four incredible people. Although one Senior Adviser offered to share his office with me, the offer was rejected. Nonetheless, I turned this plot against me into a positive situation.

However, I was shocked to learn during one of my presidential briefings that the Senior Executive had previously informed the President that I wanted to be relocated to the Ministry of Gender, and that I wasn't comfortable at State House. This was a clear manipulation of facts and abuse of position. Apparently, the President had rejected this option and asked me to continue doing my job. I could count on his fullest support as long as I carried on delivering on my mandate. It explained the desperate attempt to make me move and the offer of paying for an office out of personal funds. I wondered why a senior official would go to such extreme lengths. My only crime was being thorough in my work and an unwillingness to compromise on issues that were not in the best interest of the country, especially those affecting women's rights. My stance during the SLCDT was a warning sign that I wasn't prepared to compromise, and therefore a threat.

My reporting line to the President was clear: my briefs would be channelled through the COS. However, after I wrote my first brief, I was told it should be sent directly to the President. This was not helpful as I had no guidelines on writing presidential briefing notes and it took me approximately four hours to draft a two-paragraph note. I remember asking a young woman to check what I had written as she had experience of the system. She was extremely helpful. Again, this was another ploy to make me look incompetent and make it easier to convince the President to relocate me. Fortunately, my brief was well noted and actioned. Once I realised what was happening, I redoubled my efforts and practised writing advisory and briefing notes which I showed to a Senior Adviser for feedback. Within a month I became competent at writing advisory notes and the Senior Executive started asking me to send them through him. As I was comfortable with the current system, I told him that unless the President directed otherwise, I would continue sending my briefs directly. Naturally, this didn't go down well. However, it was his decision to let me report directly, expecting it could be my downfall. In the end it turned out to be one of my strengths.

Six months into my tenure, there was a Cabinet reshuffle following the general elections. The President had secured his second term, but there was a change in the senior leadership. I was excited and hopeful that it would herald a new beginning for me. Unfortunately, the replacement Senior Executive continued to marginalise my role. He had been briefed by his predecessor and decided to uphold the status quo. I was invited to a meeting where he proposed that I move into a new unit as Gender Specialist and the President would be informed accordingly. Again, I rejected this offer. However, I was stunned when he came out of a larger meeting and told the group that there was no need to advertise the role of Gender Specialist because I had agreed to accept the position. I was in shock, and immediately countered his claim, demanding that it was noted in the minutes of the meeting. A little later I requested to excuse myself from the meeting. I immediately wrote to the President explaining the seriousness of my situation, stating that I would be unable to deliver on my mandate under the Office of the Chief of Staff. I requested to be reassigned directly under his leadership or I would have to offer my resignation. Without any notice, the President directed the Secretary to the President to act on my reassignment with immediate effect and the letters were sent to all the necessary offices. It was a great day for me: I finally started to implement my mandate six months after I was appointed. This was a bold, but shocking, move to many in the establishment.

8
A New Role

Special Gender Adviser to the President

In January 2013, I was officially reassigned to report directly to the President under the official title Special Gender Adviser to the President with all the benefits and privileges accorded. Administratively, my role fell under the Office of the Secretary to the President. I was immediately assigned an office with budgetary support and an official car, and was able to attend meetings that were previously closed to me. The timing was perfect: the President was commencing his second term in office. It was time to prove myself.

Presenting Dr Maria Tereze De La Vega, and the delegation from Spain, to the President in 2014

The national five-year Poverty Reduction Strategic Plan (PRSP III), commonly known as the Agenda for Prosperity (A4P 2013–2018), was being developed and I requested to join the team at the Ministry of Finance. They had already agreed on seven thematic priority areas, all led by men. I quickly organised a meeting with the Ministry of Gender, UN Agencies and the ADfB to discuss the possibility of adding Gender Equality and Women's Empowerment (GEWE) as an eighth pillar. Almost everyone was pessimistic, even though they believed it was a brilliant idea. I told them I needed their support and would propose for it to be formally added to the agenda for the committee to consider and, if necessary, take it to the Minister of Finance and the President. I was determined to secure pillar eight. After two technical presentations, with a few subtle and cunning power tactics, my colleagues unanimously accepted the proposal to add the GEWE pillar and mainstream gender issues to the remaining seven. This was a huge success as it was the first time gender had gained such status in our country's plans for national development. Immediately after approval, the ADfB and UN Women funded two consultants to offer technical support for the development of pillar eight. GEWE attracted further funding from the government and development partners. The Ministry of Finance started the implementation of gender budgeting. My work plan was now guided by the A4P and the policies under pillar eight.

My role also required me to advise the Minister of Gender and to work collaboratively in achieving gender equality. However, some members from the diplomatic community felt my role was becoming too powerful and influential. They started interfering in the affairs between my office and the minister. They insinuated that at the rate at which things were progressing, it was possible that the Office of the Gender Adviser would overshadow the ministry. As it was clear that my office wasn't going to be manipulated, I knew these were disruptive tactics, especially since one individual had lost the privilege to hire presidential advisers. It wasn't too long before they were able to succeed in getting the minister to believe them. However, I paid little attention and concentrated on delivering on my mandate.

During my tenure, I accomplished some historic achievements. My office was one of only two presidential gender advisory offices within the African Union, and my office was the only one that reported directly to the President. I became the first Sierra Leonean to be nominated by the Economic Community of West African States (ECOWAS) to be elected Vice Chairperson of United Nations Economic Commission for Africa (UNECA) Bureau of Women and Development (2013–2015). Sierra Leone had never held a position since the inception of the Bureau in the 1970s. I worked closely with my fellow executives to deliver technical advice and support to member states on the Post 2015 Agenda – Common African Position (CAP 2015). The input of Sierra Leone and the evident political will from the President led to him being recognised and invited by UN Women to become one of the founding presidents for the He4She campaign, conferred Gender Champion status by UNECA and awarded the AU Gender Champion 2015.

The UN Delegation and Cherie Blair at the Presidential Lodge after paying a courtesy call on President Ernest Bai Koroma for International Women's Day 2013

Our country attracted numerous courtesy requests from globally well-respected women through embassies and organisations. I co-ordinated many of these visits, including Mrs Cherie Blair (Cherie Blair Foundation) as a special guest for International Women's Day 2013 and to launch the OWNERS business network; former Deputy Prime Minister of Spain María Teresa Fernández de la Vega to launch Women Taxi Driver's initiative; Mrs Evelyn Oputu, Managing Director, Bank of Industry Nigeria; Dr Jill Biden, wife of the former US Vice President. Dr Biden's visit was one of the highlights of my career as it gave me the privilege to work with US officials at the highest level, including the White House.

Dr Jill Biden wishing me happy birthday while visiting the President as part of her Africa tour in July 2014

As part of the national gender mainstreaming strategy, I ensured that reporting on gender accounted for 20% of performance contracts between ministries, Departments and Agencies (MDAs). This was highly successful, and we saw ministers try hard not to fail in this target. I continued to advocate and lobby the President to appoint more women in political decision-making, and some progress was made, it was fulfilling to see the appointment of the first female State Chief of Protocol. Although the President continued to appoint more women to significant positions during my tenure, I feel more could have been done. However, I learned a great deal about the influence of political parties on political appointments. I was lucky to have been appointed at my level without being a member of a political party, particularly the ruling party. I worked collaboratively with women's organisations and supported the formation, strengthening and implementation of initiatives, including female bike riders, female musicians, Women of Wanjama (WoW) and many more.

I also worked closely with traditional institutions such as the National Council of Paramount Chiefs and Sowies. I discovered that whatever I did with them had impactful and sustainable results and I involved them in all my work. In my opinion, the commitment and ownership displayed by Paramount Chiefs on development issues produced much more impressive results than some ministers could ever hope to achieve. They were trusted more than central government and things got done once action was delegated. But I noticed that these traditional leaders were not always accorded the respect they deserved. They weren't always regularly paid and some looked impoverished. Although some were politically aligned, there was a subtle move by politicians to unearth stories to marginalise some of these leaders. It was sad to see central politics deepening the divide between Paramount Chiefs, and by so doing undermining their collective power and influence in national development. I saw some of these actions as a blatant affront to their authority. During my working relationship with them, I became aware of a gradual cognitive shift among many of them to protect women's rights. We walked a slow path to empower more female Paramount Chiefs, and although much hasn't changed, progress continues. I see more support from male Chiefs towards their female colleagues than I envisaged. The thorny issue of female Paramount Chiefs was highlighted during my tenure because we constantly discussed it. I felt, and still feel like, a daughter to this institution, and I will champion them at every opportunity.

I was saddened by the way they were initially treated by the government and international community during the Ebola epidemic. I felt they were dismissed out of hand and overlooked. During the first Presidential Task Force meeting, I recommended that the government and partners strengthen the National Council of Paramount Chiefs to spearhead the progress. It was vehemently rejected, and I ended up arguing with an overzealous development partner after the meeting. Their interest was not Sierra Leone, but donor politics and superiority. It was not surprising that I was taken off the Task Force, but I was unapologetic about my actions. I decided to work with the Chiefs to see what they could do without funding. While everyone was fighting over money, our people were dying. The following week, I met with the Executive of the National Council of Paramount Chiefs at their monthly meeting at the Ministry of Local Government. I recommended that they execute an important strategy that didn't require money but would greatly contribute to ending the deadly virus nationally. As moral guarantors of tradition and culture, they had the authority to stop all initiation rites of passage within male and female secret societies. Since the initial case of Ebola was in a female traditional leader, and given the high rate of bodily contact during initiation ceremonies, this single strategy could save millions of lives. They agreed and asked me to draft a press release to that effect. I wrote the release and sent it to the Chairman for approval. Once it was edited and approved, it was for me to transmit to the national press. Two days later, I circulated the press release to journalists during a press conference on Ebola with the President at State House. This decision by the Chiefs was commendable; it brought them the much-needed attention they required to exercise leadership in tackling the menace and saving lives.

Leaving State House

Working in State House was both rewarding and challenging. I remain grateful to the former President Dr Ernest Bai Koroma for the opportunity to serve at such a senior level. I valued every moment, regardless of some of the difficult circumstances. It is well known that my role as the first Special Gender Adviser put a spotlight on gender and women's issues nationally and internationally. However, the challenges were like landmines – they could explode at any point. My success caused indignation among many men and some women, with comments such as: 'Who does she think she is? Why should she hold that position? She is not even a registered member. We were here before her.'

I was hounded both politically and professionally up on my appointment. Politically, some members of the ruling party didn't trust me to hold such a prominent position because I wasn't a party member. I was labelled as an opposition spy being planted to pass sensitive information to the main opposition party because of my tribe and region. Party activists would go to great lengths to concoct false stories about official activities and pass them on to their internal circle. On the other hand, the opposition party viewed me as selling out for accepting the job, even though I wasn't even a member of their party. A leading newspaper went further and blamed me for being responsible for granting the Executive Representative of the Secretary-General a persona non grata status, something I knew nothing about while at the UN. It became so bad that the newspaper even reported that my degrees were fake. Some women were upset that the President hadn't talked to them first prior to my appointment, as they knew better qualified people. Some even refused to talk or work with me. It was really disheartening to experience this, but today I can understand some of these sentiments. I was completely oblivious to the political struggle women faced to get into political leadership, because my journey had been basically seamless. I was someone who happened to be at the right place at the right time and willing to seize opportunities when they arose. I was highly qualified for the job and was proactive in engaging directly with the President over the cause of gender and women's rights.

My position and career progress posed a huge threat to some ministers, and they went overboard to undermine my authority both officially and politically. Although other advisers faced similar predicaments, my treatment was particularly overt. One person would refuse to attend partner meetings if I was on the programme. He spearheaded the 'golden girl' rumour that I was sleeping with the President and this was the reason for my remarkable success. It became so bad that I went to the President in tears at this deliberate character assassination; he encouraged me to stay strong and shared similar stories of being accused of sleeping with every woman he appointed. The President found this conduct towards me and others very disappointing because it could influence whether he appointed a woman or not.

After three years it became too much and I was contemplating leaving my job to pursue something else. I had discussed this with one of the President's close aides and hadn't even bothered to request my contract renewal before I went on a month's leave. While on leave, I was asked to accompany the Minister of Foreign Affairs on his campaign for the presidency of the ADfB because I was part of the team. We went to London, the Hague and Copenhagen. My presence at the meetings was greatly appreciated by the host countries, especially Denmark where the Foreign Minister singled out Sierra Leone for being so gender responsive during the process. At the end of the trip, I went to Amsterdam to continue my holiday with my friend Mariam, and I received a message from a colleague saying that my contract wasn't going to be renewed and that the Ministry of Finance had the memo. I told him that I hadn't been informed but would contact the Secretary to the President for confirmation. Although I was relieved on some level, I hadn't expected this sudden turn of events, especially as I hadn't done anything administratively wrong. I was also relieved that I hadn't been sacked as that would have appeared as an official news item.

When I got to London, there was an email from the Secretary to the President who had been trying to reach me by phone. Because I had left my laptop in

London, I hadn't had access to work emails. When I called and asked what had happened, he told me the President hadn't given a reason. He was also baffled and had wanted to hear from me. I found it difficult breaking the news to my family and friends, but I felt hugely supported. When I returned to Freetown to resume work, the news was already making the rounds, but no one had the back story. I initially thought the aide might have told the President about our conversation, but he said that wasn't the case. At the end of my tenure, I had an exit briefing with the President. I thanked him for the opportunity to serve my country under his leadership and presented my handover notes. I remained calm even though some senior government officials had encouraged me to apologise; one even suggested falling on the floor and crying so that he would reverse his decision. I couldn't understand why I should make a nuisance of myself, especially as I hadn't been found wanting in any way. It would be professionally unethical and I would not humiliate myself like that.

At the end of the briefing, the President looked sad:

'I know you are wondering why I have decided to conclude your assignment. Let me first assure you that you are one of my most professional, passionate and committed staff and I have confidence in your work. But I must protect you and my decision was taken in that regard. I intend to reassign you to another

position, and I will shortly give the announce-
ment. I need to get you out of here, you will
one day understand why. Please take all the
time you need and complete what you need
to do. You are welcome to come here or to the
Presidential Lodge at any time, and keep the
communication lines open. You will hear from
me shortly. Thank you for your excellent work
so far.'

When I came out of his office everyone, including
the Vice President who was just going in to see the
President, wanted to know the outcome of our discussions. I just said that I didn't cry or apologise and that
I was happy with the President's decision. They all
looked baffled. A few days later, a senior official in the
presidency told me that someone came while I was on
leave and threatened to resign over an advisory note
from me that the President had acted on. When any
gender-related issues reached the President, I would
usually be asked to write an advisory note or have
a meeting to guide his response. The issue in question involved three ministers; two respected and supported the recommendations. However, the third
reacted aggressively and threatened to resign. This
was later confirmed by an elderly lady who overheard
a conversation at the Vice President's residence. She
told me that the people in the compound were saying that the Vice President had advised the President
to remove me from State House to stop the minister
from resigning. The woman was sad to hear what

was going on. Although I had no reason to doubt the validity of this account, I was still sceptical about apportioning blame. However, the elder brother of the relevant minister phoned one female leader in my district to boast about his part in all this. It was a deliberate attempt to taunt and provoke her. I told her not to react but to accept what the President had shared with me.

I left State House three weeks after my contract ended and refused to grant any interviews to the press. This just intensified the rumours and resulted in a misinformed video that was politically motivated. However, despite the President's promise and an apology from a senior official in his political party, I wasn't reassigned to another government position.

In the meantime, the waiting to hear caused me serious financial constraints; I didn't want to accept another job while waiting to be re-appointed. I was conscious that the President wouldn't take kindly to job hunting or receiving requests for references when he had asked me to wait. Sometimes it made me angry. I had my own issues to deal with: my daughter was at university and I was running out of funds. It was tough as I had only my monthly salary to rely on. Although things were a bit difficult while waiting, I received a huge amount of goodwill from people, especially women. A woman would call to check on me and then invite me to lunch or dinner. When I left, they would smile and hand me an envelope filled with dollars.

Without asking, fellow women supported me financially for nearly a year. They would send me wine, champagne, buy me air tickets and take me out to dinner overseas. You couldn't tell that I wasn't earning because these women stood by me to make me financially comfortable. Traditional women would send me gallons of palm oil, fish and agricultural products which I would end up sharing. I felt appreciated and loved by other women. I owe my sanity to the women of Sierra Leone. It was equally heartening to think that it was a young woman who had opened the door for me to pursue an Executive Master of Public Administration and gain a Pentland Scholarship. Eventually I got the break I really wanted from the government, which led me to gain further professional and academic knowledge.

9
Building Women's Leadership

Women of Wanjama (WoW)

My experience in setting up the Sowie Councils encouraged me to take a lead in supporting the formation of other women's groups to foster solidarity. Although there were many women's groups, including the umbrella Women's Forum, I noticed that solidarity was a bit thin on the ground. Multiple conflicting interests and politics have been key divisive factors and often cause for some groups to be ineffective. I wanted to create organisations and promote shared and collective leadership by example. Community organising was the natural starting point for me. The Sowie Council Head from my district of birth had requested that I bring all the women together as I had done with other organisations.

At first it seemed like an impossible task; the district was highly politically divided and every objective was politicised. But I agreed to the challenge and called a women's meeting to test the atmosphere. To my greatest surprise, there was a huge turnout of women from all walks of life. I had thought of a name that would be empowering and owned by the women. Although I was born in the district, I had only spent a short time there as a child when I visited my grandparents. I really wanted the women to take ownership of the process because I was based in Freetown where I would be strategically supporting the growth of the organisation and fundraising. The people of Pujehun also refer to the area as Wanjama and the name I came up with was Women of Wanjama (WoW). The name was an immediate hit, and the women would start chanting 'WoW WoW WoW' every time we said Women of Wanjama. In March 2014, two months after the inaugural meeting, WoW hosted the President at a pre-International Women's Day Dinner in Pujehun. It was a historic event and created a prominent national platform for the group. WoW has become the leading women's organisation in the district and is routinely included in all development planning. Although I am Chairperson, the administration of the organisation remains firmly in the hands of the District Executive led by the Deputy Chairperson. One key mandate that WoW has delivered on is supporting women's leadership. WoW played a key role in the election of the first female Paramount Chief Member of Parliament and recently campaigned to get one of the youngest female Paramount Chiefs elected. The organisation lobbied the current government to appoint one of our members to a senior leadership position after she narrowly lost by two votes for the District Chairperson seat. Other initiatives have included awareness of sexual and gender-based violence, district-wide awareness on ending Ebola, and agriculture and animal husbandry to promote women's economic empowerment. I recently announced my intention to step down as Chairperson because the organisation has been doing very well without a great deal of input from me.

United for Humanity

A few months after leaving State House, I renewed the registration of United for Humanity which we formed to raise funds for the Haiti earthquake in 2010. Its focus would be on ending sexual violence, addressing traditional rites of passage for girls and promoting women's political empowerment. These three issues had featured heavily in my roles at the UN and in government. I was keen to work with other civil society organisations to constructively engage policymakers to act. I had meetings with Paramount Chiefs and other female traditional leaders, including Sowies, about strengthening our existing partnership. My aim was to use our own people and our own financial resources to deal with issues. I believe this is the best way to address social issues as it promotes ownership and sustainability, and discourages reliance on external donor support.

I launched a Call to Action event to support the establishment of a fund for survivors of sexual violence. To show my commitment, I donated approximately five acres of land in Pujehun for the construction of a women's village as a transitional home for victims and survivors. This was in response to the limited availability of places of refuge nationally. The village is intended to be a one-stop shop, providing psychological, medical and legal services within a confidential and safe setting. Donations in kind and cash were used for manufacturing concrete blocks for fencing, clearing and other related costs to securing the land. I reached out to local dignitaries to support the initiative, but nobody has yet delivered on their promises. Although I have been unable to raise enough funds to build the village, I remain optimistic that my dream of establishing this vital initiative will be actualised.

Southern Province Women's Net

Given the lack of collaboration between women's organisations, and the negative impact this had on women's empowerment, I decided to replicate the Women of Wanjama (WoW) model to connect women from all walks of life in the Southern Province. The common goal would be to achieve gender equality. WoW had survived vigorous attacks from stakeholders, including other women, to become the most prominent women's organisation in Pujehun. Nationally, the group is well known and praised by the former and current administrations, but there was a lack of representation of women from the South in the Koroma All People's Congress Party-led administration. I was among only a handful of women who were fortunate enough to serve during their ten-year regime.

I found this lack of representation extremely negative for promoting women and girls' empowerment. I wanted to know why men from the region had important political appointments and top jobs in the Civil Service, but hardly any women did. I discussed the issue with the President and Vice President and was told that women from the South were turning down appointments because of their strong political party convictions. This statement was confirmed by some of the key female members of the main opposition party; men were more willing to leave their parties to work with the ruling government. I had personally tried to promote a few women, but they told me that it wasn't just party loyalty; a bigger consideration was their lack of agency. They needed the approval of their husbands to make the decision. I found this equally disturbing and decided to form the Southern Province Women's Network (SProWNet) representing the four districts (Bo, Bonthe, Moyamba and Pujehun) to address some of these issues. I reached out to female acquaintances from all walks of life and political parties to join me in solidarity. Many removed their political lenses and accepted to be part of the organisation.

From its inception in July 2016, it was mainly a WhatsApp group. There were sceptics who thought I was trying to mobilise political support for me and my political party. I expected scepticism and had already developed mental resilience and constructive responses based on the WoW experience. In November 2016, we held our first meeting and the turnout was impressive. The women decided that we should set up an interim Executive to lead the affairs of the organisation and I was nominated to serve as Founding Chairperson. It was a humbling, but rather huge, responsibility to leading Paramount Chiefs, senior Parliamentarians and other eminent women from the region. I knew it wasn't going to be an easy job. My collective leadership style was alien to some members of the team, but we forged ahead and made progress. We registered the organisation and one of our talented members, Fatou Wurie, kindly designed our logo. We solicited the support of another woman, Toodi Stronge, to help us with the constitution. It was tough, but we completed the requirements to formalise the organisation. However, in May 2017 I was awarded a scholarship to pursue a Joint EMPA at NYU and UCL which meant being away for a year. The Public Relations Officer (PRO) Gertrude Karimu said that we needed to launch the organisation. I wasn't keen due to the lack of commitment from members and the fact that I was planning to go to New York. But she insisted; not launching the organisation would be a missed opportunity. She indicated that it would be a deliberate failure for me to give up as no one else could lead the process. I accepted her rebuke and went into action. We agreed on a mini launch as a strategy to regroup and keep our collective aspirations alive. Her advice was invaluable and a turning point for SProWNet because the organisation survived despite the fact that the commitment was still low. In August 2017, a day before I departed to America, we had a successful pre-launch which was well attended by various dignitaries, including the then Hon Minister of Social Welfare, Gender and Children's Affairs. We opened a bank account and undertook some small events to promote our visibility nationally. The key aim of the organisation is to promote and protect women and girls from the region, using all strategies, including human capital, to contribute to national development.

In the general elections in March 2018, the opposition party won power. Our membership was approximately 90% women from the opposition party, but we were deliberate in keeping politics out of the forum. We were committed as an organisation to promoting our members regardless of their politics. We had banned all forms of politicking as it would undermine our existence and credibility. Our leadership was put to the test: members tried to flaunt the rules and impose political dialogue. We fought this vigorously and some members left, but we knew we had to stand firm. As the new government settled into power, some of our members started to be appointed into government positions. SProWNet moved from having only one appointed woman in the previous administration to several appointees. This included a ministerial position, commissioners and board members. Although we saw a drastic reduction of female MPs, we now have the only two female Paramount Chief Members of Parliament (PCMP). The only woman to retain her parliamentary seat is now the most senior female law maker and President of the Female Parliamentary Caucus. Our organisation boasts of professionals from diverse backgrounds: businesswomen, female political leaders from different political parties, civil society leaders, human rights defenders, including the Chairperson of the Human Rights Commission.

The SProWNet initiative has created an impact and motivated other women from other regions to form similar networks, including the Northern Region Women's Network (NReWN) and Eastern Region Women's Network (EReWN). After successfully leading the organisation for three years, I decided to step down to pursue my own political ambitions. The membership requested that I should oversee the official launching and first Annual General Meeting (AGM) to usher in a new administration. I accepted and worked hard with my Executive to fulfil both obligations, even though I was unable to attend the AGM due to medical reasons. We handed over the organisation with a larger, stronger membership and sound financial status. SProWNet is nationally known as one of the key women's organisations in the country and we continue to expand, building strong partnerships with the government, civil society organisations, women's groups and international agencies for national development.

Deputy Leader of the Unity Party

There are very few female leaders in political parties in Sierra Leone. The two main political parties have women's wings, which I find disturbing on many levels. The woman who leads the wing holds significant power. She is usually strongly aligned to the male-dominated political hierarchy. Her influence is so powerful that women who are not in agreement with her often suffer politically, as they may be sidelined for political party symbols and other political appointments. Interestingly, the Presidents of the women's wings are often in conflict with the First Ladies because of their close working relationships with the Presidents. Politicians can use this situation to exacerbate the conflict between these two powerful women, and female party members end up being in rival camps. This is one of the most destructive strategies in undermining women's political empowerment in Africa.

When I saw a woman standing for president from the newly founded Unity Party in the 2018 general elections, I was intrigued and wanted to meet her, even though I am a member of the All People's Congress. I reached out to her over national radio, but as I needed to return to UCL in London, I could only speak to her briefly. I assured her that I would join her at some point in my political journey when I finally returned home. Although she didn't perform well in the polls, she stood firm and didn't compromise her position by joining any of the other parties. When my party lost the general elections, I decided it was time to consider joining the Unity Party.

In May 2018 after graduating from NYU, I called Femi Claudius Cole to congratulate her on her resilience in surviving the harsh terrain of the general elections. She was very pleased to hear from me as she was going through one of the lowest moments in her life. She felt that she hadn't been supported by her fellow women, but recognised that the party had only come into existence six months prior to the general elections. I told her that I would like to join her party, but I needed a prominent role that would create a visible impact. Femi was delighted and we agreed to meet in Freetown the following month so she could consult her membership on possible positions. When we met in Freetown, she informed me that the Deputy Leader position was available and that she would like to propose me to the membership but required my consent. As this was going to make the news headlines, I told her that if the membership agreed, I would need to resign from my current party. Once I was informed of the agreement, I resigned – much to the surprise of many in the All People's Congress. I knew my growth potential in the APC was limited, based on my experiences while serving as Gender Adviser to the President. Once the formalities were completed, I was invited to the Unity Party office to officially join the party and accept the position of Deputy Chairperson/ Leader. I officially announced my appointment on my Facebook page using the hashtag #WomenWillWin.

Rugby

Although I engaged in sport in secondary school and led my school to numerous victories, I didn't pursue it in adult life. Football is the most popular sport in Sierra Leone, but I am not a huge fan. I don't support a team or follow any of the world-famous clubs. However, when I was on my Pentland Scholarship I became interested in rugby and immediately saw its possibilities. In January 2019, I posted an enquiry about the status of rugby in Sierra Leone. Just a few people responded, while others ridiculed the notion of a national rugby team. It turned out that, since the 1970s, Sierra Leone had a rich history of the game, with an active national team and regional associations. Unfortunately, the game wasn't popular due to lack of governance and poor leadership. The President of the Sierra Leone Rugby Union (SLRU) contacted me and after a lengthy discussion I was invited to become a board member. Although I wasn't sure how well I would fit in, I realised it was an ideal platform to solicit support from the Pentland Group.

The Pentland Group was a key sponsor of the Rugby World Cup 2019 and the famous Canterbury rugby brand is part of the Pentland family. I contacted the Chairman of Pentland, Stephen Rubin, informed him of my appointment to the Board of the SLRU and told him that I needed some help to understand the game. He was delighted and immediately requested that the head of Canterbury meet with me to discuss my request. The meeting was very productive and resulted in a shared vision to promote women's rugby in Sierra Leone. A few days later, the company invited me to Twickenham to watch the England v France game from the Canterbury booth. This new interest was becoming serious. I live streamed the game on Facebook and my friends were surprised at their instant connection with the game. It was time for me to return to Sierra Leone to find out first-hand the real state of rugby back home. Before my departure, I got a call from Pentland who wanted to donate 150 Canterbury jerseys to the SLRU. I was overcome with gratitude, as was the President of SLRU, who was very emotional when he received the news.

On my return, I found out that there were no legal structures in place to promote the growth of the game. This came as a slight shock, especially as Pentland had made some vital introductions which could help improve the status of rugby in Sierra Leone, nationally and internationally. They had great expectations from me and I wasn't going to disappoint them after the exceptional support they had already shown SLRU. I asked a few women to join me in promoting women's rugby and we established the Women's Rugby Advisory Committee of SLRU. World Rugby had a robust programme to promote gender equality and had an ambitious Forward Development Plan to accelerate the global development of women in rugby. I wanted to align our activities to these strategies.

I proposed four other women from our newly established Women's Committee to join the SLRU board and fortunately there was no opposition. In reality, a formal board did not exist, despite several people being given appointments by the President. The first board meeting was called, and I was unanimously elected Board Chairperson. The responsibilities were huge as the entire SLRU needed an overhaul. We had five women and four men on the board, and this was great news as we made instant history worldwide. The gender formation of the SLRU attracted Women's Rugby who wanted to run an in-depth article on our progress to find out how we managed to have more women than men on our board. After the story was published, Rugby Africa – the administrative body for rugby union in the continent of Africa – contacted the SLRU President to confirm what they had read. Our relationship was poised to get back on track.

Some members of the original Executive were unhappy at what was happening at SLRU, especially as some members of the Women's Committee held two positions, including the important post of Treasurer. We insisted that the SLRU be formally registered with the Corporate Affairs Commission after drafting a legally binding constitution, which would allow us to open bank accounts. This restructuring was certainly not expected and some men on the Executive decided to undermine the process. Despite these difficulties the board, coaches, players and Women's Committee insisted on the restructuring, including calling for an AGM to usher in a new Executive. The attitude and behaviour of some of the men didn't come as a surprise and I was ready to constructively deal with the situation. This is an ongoing process. Kent Cricket Club recently donated to the SLRU kits, including balls, shorts, mouthguards and cones. This level of support and solidarity is unprecedented and both our organisations have pledged to strengthen it.

10
Women Will Win

#WomenWillWin

When I left the Office of the President in 2015, I was furious at the way women were perceived and treated by the political elite in Sierra Leone. The constant humiliation, bullying and lies made up to impede women's leadership were disturbing and discouraging. Every time a woman was appointed or did well, men became threatened and found ways of sabotaging them. There were always excuses for why women had to take a back seat. Sexual harassment and intimidation were the norm. Some of my most distressing memories include consoling a female Deputy Minister who was sidelined and bullied by her male boss; local government candidates who were sexually harassed for political party symbols to contest the 2012 elections; and a senior civil servant who was similarly abused by a party stalwart because she had instituted reforms around access to the President.

Young women continue to be solicited by politicians for sexual favours in exchange for financial support. There was an example of a young university student who reported being raped by a Deputy Minister who was later sacked, tried, acquitted and reinstated to a different ministry. Meanwhile the young woman had to flee the country because our justice system had failed her. This case was brought to my attention by the Consultant Judge who was initially assigned to her case. He was disgusted and openly told me how senior politicians from the 'alleged' rapist's district constantly called him to try to influence the case, which he refused to do. One morning he found out that the case file had been reassigned to another judge who was later rewarded with a promotion.

I personally experienced organised intimidation by fellow senior public officials which led to my contract not being renewed by the presidency. I saw first-hand how a female minister was hounded; I also happened to be in the room full of men and the President when they decided her fate. I knew she would not survive the weekend: she was sacked.

These experiences showed me how entrenched in our society is the battle to impede women's empowerment. It has prepared me for a lifetime's commitment to support women win the war for equal power. I created #WomenWillWin and decided to show how we could collectively achieve this through some of my current initiatives, using my own experiences as a baseline.

The level of reported sexual violence continues to rise despite our strong legal framework, including the revised Sexual Offences Act 2019. Victims and survivors were optimistic when the new administration took an unprecedented political stance and declared sexual and gender-based violence a national emergency. However, a year later cases are on the increase and political will seems to be slowly fading. Many organisations have also scaled down their robust campaigns on this issue; some quietly distanced themselves from certain cases depending on their political interests. Nationally, the country seems to be reactive. When a case of sexual violence emerges, there is increased social media outrage but that gradually evaporates and is forgotten. This means that victims and survivors must cope on their own as there are no medium- or long-term support systems. In my opinion, women and girls continue to lose the case against impunity on sexual violence as the entire system is riddled with blatant impediments to justice.

Being a rape survivor, I decided to use my own story and platform to raise awareness on ending rape in Sierra Leone. I decided to create the 50th Speaker Series to engage fifty schools in strategies to prevent rape. This was also a personal journey in my own healing process to bring closure to my ordeal which I had lived with for over thirty-five years. I had no money and relied on the goodwill of friends and family to implement the programme. I reached out to a small network of people for support and I was fortunate to receive a proactive response. One of Africa's leading mobile companies, Africell, agreed to become my main corporate sponsor and led the marketing and communications side of my campaign. Jill and Co slashed their fees to 50% for both their photo and filming services. 'Sierra Eye', a female-led magazine, also threw in their financial support. However, the initial financial support came from Michala Mackay to launch the programme at her alma mater, St Joseph's Secondary School. She also gave me the greatest confidence to take the series forward. Close friends, including Sinkarie Sesay, Josephine Dauda and Femi Claudius Cole, were with me at the launch at St Joseph's to provide welcome support. It was an emotional day and I was in tears before going on stage, but the students were extremely supportive and we completed the programme successfully. It convinced me that I had embarked on a meaningful journey.

The 50th Speaker Series has reached approximately thirteen thousand students in Sierra Leone. Although the series was initially aimed at secondary schools, a few primary schools have also benefited from the programme and students have spoken openly about their issues on sexual violence. There has been a great deal of mutual empathy between me and the students. However, my biggest challenge came after I had spoken to students of the Holy Rosary Junior Secondary School. Two young girls chased after me at the end and asked why I wasn't naming my perpetrator – the Reverend. They asked whether I was just telling a story, or if was it real. They said that if I wanted them to tell me or others the names of those who had violated them, I should name mine also. This was a strong indictment and required an instant response. I assured them that I would name my perpetrators in future programmes.

Evaluate

The following morning when I was addressing the students at my alma mater, the Methodist Secondary School in Kenema, I revealed the name of the Reverend who had raped me. I felt relieved and I told the school that I didn't blame them; they were not responsible for the Reverend's actions. It was a tough process and afterwards I went to the church to talk to the current Reverend. It was an extremely difficult and emotional day, but I felt as though a burden had lifted. Although I never allowed the series to be filmed live, I made an exception that day and my story was all over social media. The Reverend also appeared on social media trying to deny it, but I rebutted him with further email evidence. I received an unprecedented number of phone calls, messages and social media posts in support of my stance. Women called me, crying and sharing their long-kept secret stories of rape and other sexual abuse. There were inevitably a few people who decided to discredit my story, while others questioned the timing. However, I was consoled by the massive outpouring of support and I continued the series with more strength.

I was invited to Ghana by the Girls Empowerment Movement (GEM) as a special guest to share my story at one of their schools. I found similar stories of sexual abuse against girls and a comparable level of injustice, partly due to stigma, a culture of silence and poverty. It was painful when a young girl asked to speak to me privately to share how she had been raped by a judge. She looked just like me at fifteen and had been dealing with her trauma since she was thirteen. She told me that all she wanted was justice and I passed this matter on to the organisation to follow up because I was powerless to help her. I started asking myself whether I should continue; the process was opening wounds for children who had no support system. These were difficult times emotionally.

When I resumed the series in Sierra Leone, I decided to explore the possibility of setting up counselling rooms in schools to support at-risk girls and victims of sexual abuse. The schools approved of the idea and felt it was a practical and feasible way of supporting girls. However, I only had enough funding to finish my series, but I continue to explore how we can establish these counselling rooms. Some businesses and individuals pulled out from supporting the initiative because they didn't want to upset the political establishment. It has been an eye opener, but my motivation to continue remains strong. I will use personal funds, including the proceeds from my book, to support the completion of the 50th Speaker Series and to establish the counselling rooms.

In December 2019, I was invited by the Women's Network of the London School of Economics School of Public Policy during the '16 Days of Activism against Gender-Based Violence' as a keynote speaker to speak about the 50th Speaker Series. Women should come together to support each other whatever differences we may have. The cause of women's empowerment should transcend our personal agendas. Without collective leadership and ownership to own and rule our stories, we will continue to be victimised. I have used my ordeal to strengthen my coping mechanisms and support other women and girls come to terms with their trauma. We need one another to succeed at all levels and we can do this through the winning formula of the three Cs: Community, Connecting, Celebrating.

Community: I see women as a global community with shared experiences of joy and pain. We have been fighting independently in sub communities for similar issues and for our human rights. There have been global women's rights icons and collective gatherings working together to create frameworks that will enable us to succeed in winning our common struggles. We must win by consolidating our gains.

Connecting: We cannot win in isolation, no matter how hard we try. Women must share stories and strategies by connecting our global communities. We are already doing that, and social media has made it easier, but billions of women do not have access to the bare necessities, let alone the internet. Women must first bridge the gap locally by being inclusive across educational, economical, generational and cultural spectrums. Connectivity is about our shared pain, joy and commitment to solve our problems together. The pain women share has no boundaries; we must therefore win without borders.

Celebrating: Women are good at amplifying and connecting our struggles, but we don't usually celebrate as a community when we win. We must showcase our successes internationally without borders so that other women can learn. From the village to the presidency we must celebrate women to strengthen our sisterhood. Our Community must Connect at least one billion women across borders to Celebrate using the #WomenWillWin campaign. Together we can take charge to go for what we want!

Conclusion

Lived experience

Life has been a cocktail of experiences and I am comfortable with the woman I have become. The challenges in my life have created opportunities for me to make meaningful life decisions. Over the years, my resilience has been strengthened as a result of pain and trauma. A key factor has been how I have managed situations to bring closure on a variety of issues. I see challenges as a growth pole and success in overcoming them depends on your interpretation of the situation.

As a child I didn't grow up knowing or understanding love. I was never lucky enough to experience it. What I learned as love from my parents is known as abuse today; but I don't blame my parents. As a child it was normal to be beaten, although some of the harsh treatment I received has stayed with me in my adulthood. I didn't feel listened to at home, but I got that attention in school. I felt more valued in school because my teachers believed in me, and I only ever received one reprimand for wearing drop earrings to school. Those gold earrings were a gift from my mother and when I saw the teacher destroy them, it was not only heart-breaking but it made me resentful towards the teacher. I was only able to resolve this issue recently when I met the teacher again. She told me that she had only acted in my best interest. As she beamed with pride at the woman I have become, I was able to understand her.

However, the repercussions of her actions had a trickle-down effect on my home front. I was beaten mercilessly by my mother. There was so much anger in the punishment meted out to me; I became resilient to pain. I had to do better for my mother; she bought me everything I needed for school, including extra uniforms and school supplies. I was a neat child and wore nice clothes but I was broken inside. I couldn't connect the mother who beat me and the one who bought everything I needed, so I accepted both. It is possible my mother truly loved me, but she couldn't accept that I felt different and this has been a contentious issue between us. What is not in doubt is my love and devotion to her; I chose to be a very different mother to my own daughter. My father was the same; I simply felt insecure around him. He was a disciplinarian and his word was always final, but I experienced a softer Papa who apologised to me in 1993 before I left for the United Kingdom. Sadly, it was the last conversation we had before he passed away. I took solace from the fact that we managed to resolve some of my burning childhood issues and he gave me some gold and little diamonds from the mines. I miss him now more than ever. Although I had a difficult childhood, I don't believe that my parents meant to abuse me or had a deliberate agenda to harm me. Their era was different, and I never had the chance to understand what it was like for them as children; maybe that might throw some light on their actions. What came out of my childhood experience was my determination to be a different mother to my daughter and to manage my relationship with my ex-husband. I didn't want my daughter to suffer the consequences of my own experience and I hope that I have lived up to her expectations; only she can tell me in the future.

Marriage has been a controversial issue for me. I have limited memories of living with both parents, but I spent some time with my father and stepmother. Papa loved his wife and treated her like a queen. Naturally, I was jealous, especially as I felt that I always came second. But he was a considerate husband. My mother was determined to remain single and protected us from any of the men who came into her life. She was in charge of all decisions regarding her children and any man who tried to interfere would have to leave. This unusual aspect of her parenting earned her the love and respect of her children. I grew up with a woman with a can-do attitude, who was very cautious towards the prospect of any further marriages. I believe she was worried about the impact of stepparenting on her children and was determined to keep us with her at all costs. I was influenced by her attitude and it's why I don't look on marriage as most people do. I believe in the institution of marriage, but it has to be an equal partnership with love, trust and mutual respect. I didn't want a contentious divorce, nor was I concerned about material gain. Psychological wellbeing and peace of mind were the biggest factors and have always played a major part in my decision-making. You have to be comfortable with the decisions you make in life. You are the only person who understands the impact. Although consulting people and listening to advice are great, the ultimate decision lies with you because you have to live with it.

I have always lived my life challenging the status quo. From being different in my parents' eyes to challenging societal norms and practices. I am not afraid of the consequences of my decisions because there is always an opportunity to make life better. I became the woman I envisaged despite family, friends and societal expectations of me. My motivation is to show the other side of status quo and how it's mostly good. I am an outspoken woman in a culture that tries very hard to silence critical womens' voices. As a child, I would always question things that didn't make sense to me;

sometimes I would get explanations, but I refused to be silenced. I challenged the notion of boys being better than girls by competing for everything, including opting for subjects that were meant for boys, such as agriculture. I led my school against the boys' school in debates and won. It made me a target for insults, but I always responded politely.

As an adult, I have been a passionate activist on violence against women and girls, especially rape and unsafe abortions. By sharing my personal experiences around these issues, I intentionally disrupted the status quo of a culture of silence. Thousands of women and girls have told me that I have given them the confidence to deal with their situations and some are now openly talking about their experiences. I always respect the law and act accordingly. Undertaking extensive background research before I speak on an issue is one of my strongest assets. If I am wrong, I concede and apologise if necessary. The bottom line is that what I do must serve a bigger purpose for humanity.

Lessons learned

I have learned that the purpose of life is different for everyone. My purpose has changed as I progress through life and my priorities have changed too. The things I found important in my thirties don't hold the same value to me at fifty. People used to say this, but my younger self didn't understand it. What has stayed constant is my willingness to adapt and make the best of every situation. I have learned to take decisive action and follow through with what I am comfortable with. Basically, I have lived life knowing that others are passengers in my journey and that I am the driver.

When I revealed the person who raped me, many people wanted me to take him to court, but that wasn't right for me. I knew that I was telling the truth and threw the burden of legal redress over to him. By sharing my truth publicly and standing by what I said, that was my way of bringing closure to a dark episode in my life. My health improved, I felt psychologically stronger and for the first time in my life, I felt I could truly love someone. I didn't want to go to court; it wasn't my priority, although I was prepared to go if necessary. It was as though I had handed over all the shame and powerlessness I had felt. Now the burden was his to untangle.

I have learned to accept my mistakes and take responsibility to be better. I have never held grudges, and forgiving wrongs has helped me grow physically, psychologically and spiritually. Accepting my reality has helped me tap into opportunities; I don't consider challenges as failures. I do get things wrong, but I learn from those who know better. Arrogance is the greatest recipe for failure because it doesn't allow for self-reflection. I have waged head-on war against insecurity because I almost drowned in depression and nearly suffered a stroke at twenty-nine. The experience taught me to cleanse my mind rather than overload it with more pain out of pride and fear. It also showed me that, in the end, people will accept and respect your decisions because they are your life choices to own and control.

Letter to my younger self

Dear Naasu

You are one of the most resilient young women I have known in my entire life. Despite your past and current challenges, you continue to be strong, focused and committed to doing not only the best for you, but for others, especially your family. The sacrifices you continue to make to support your mother and siblings to escape poverty is commendable. I realise that life hasn't always been easy, but you always look gracious despite your pain. I sometimes wonder how you do it. How great would it be if your brain could be studied to understand how you manage situations to overcome the constant battles you fight? Indeed, you are a fighter and the commando of your life.

It is interesting how much you are misunderstood by family and friends, but you are deliberate about keeping it that way because it gives you power over your story. People choose to make assumptions rather than engage with you; not even your mother understands you, but she believes she does and gets angry for getting it wrong. Despite your outward confidence, you are very private and reticent about many things. It makes sense to hold back because you feel there is an untold story about your childhood that no one has revealed. There are clearly some unanswered questions, but no one is ready to give you the answers. Maybe, one day, you will find out by yourself. Naasu, you are completely self-sufficient – you know yourself.

Sometimes I wonder why you don't get excited about boyfriends like your contemporaries, but I understand that you have been betrayed by men you had trusted, making it difficult to truly commit to anyone. You find it a relief ending relationships because you always try to exhaust your time and love for that person, whatever the nature of you friendship. You are kind, generous, loving and loyal, but extremely inflexible with betrayal. Sometimes I honestly wish you could be more relaxed about this because getting you out of your shell involves learning a whole new discipline. You are a fine and honest young lady with great potential, but you have been extremely hard on yourself in order to achieve your best. You set your own life trajectory; it's interesting how effortlessly you plan, organise and execute things in your head without giving the slightest intimation to others. My God, you love it when you surprise yourself and people around you. You enjoy the biggest laughs when you experience those 'I did it' moments.

Many people admire you and some genuinely want you to succeed, and support whatever you choose to do. However, your very existence seems to upset some people without you really understanding why. You seem to be an enigma; some of your family are upset at your success because your mother's children were not expected to turn out like you. Their 'rudeness', as you fondly describe it, has been your greatest motivation to succeed and remove any social stigma from your family. This has been a lifelong ambition and, guess what, you have achieved it. You have supported and motivated your siblings to go on to higher education and independence, and your mother is no longer looked down upon.

You have done well as a mother, wife, entrepreneur and educated woman. You came out of your divorce with a smile on your face. The amount you achieved in your younger years deserves praise. I know you are highly driven, but I just wish you could relax and be a bit more selfish with your time. Despite everything you have been through, you remain calm and resilient in your pursuit to make the world a better place. I am enormously proud of you – stay strong. And please say yes when the time comes.

Lots of love
Mature Naasu

Acknowledgements

Fifty years of my life have involved living and dealing with many people; this book would not have been possible without acknowledging the support of many of them. Without my parents and grandparents, I wouldn't be who I am today. My late father Augustine Karimu Kamanda who instilled the discipline and fearlessness in me to pursue what I want. I miss him badly – thank you in heaven, Papa. My mother is a complex woman, but her determination to stand her ground to make sure I learned the hard way nurtured my resilience. Thank you mother for giving me the roadmap to living an independent life. I thank all my late grandparents for their loving care.

My greatest achievement is being a mother to JJ. Since birth she has challenged me to be better, wiser and more loving. Because of her, I am able to understand the meaning of unconditional love. Thank you for being a wonderful support system through everything and encouraging me to write this book.

My siblings Naasu II, Patrick and Feimata have been my companions in life. Through you, I learned to be a leader – an experience that has greatly impacted my life. I am possibly not the easiest big sister in the world but thank you for always being loving and respectful. I learned and practised patience being a sibling leader.

This book would have been impossible without the strong support of some incredible people who believed in me. My friend and sister Aisha Paparella, my partner in all things possible, thank you for being a strong pillar of support. I don't even know how you got your lovely husband Brook to put up with us – thank you Brook for letting me take over your home while in London. Special thanks to Port Loko Prince for believing in everything I do and stand for. Your guidance and support over the years have been a stabiliser across the spectrum. To my dearest baby sister and clone Hawa Marriot; your love and support gave me the steam to finally roll into action. You are the self-esteem booster; thank you and your lovely family for your unconditional love. Zainab Bashir, alias mummy, you are a voice of truth because you say it as it is with zero sugar coating. Your authentic counsel over the years has been lifesaving. Thank you for always pushing me to do the best I can and investing in my book project. Haja Ma Suaffie, what would I do without you? My sanity in Sierra Leone is partly dependent on your motherly interventions. You turn my emotional volume down. Your spiritual strength has a huge impact on my life. Thank you for being my prayer warrior. You are a blessing, the head prefect of encouragement. My friends Stefan, Jonny and all my backers who contributed through my crowdfunding site to make this a reality – thank you and I remain grateful. Special recognition to the CEO of Sea Coach Express for supporting the first donations of books in schools.

Professor Albert Weale, your mentorship gave me the confidence to finally write my book. For a year you would remind and prod me to get on with it. Your encouragement was timely. I am terribly proud to be the first Pentland Scholar to become an author. Special thanks to Mr Stephen Rubin and the Pentland family for granting me the opportunity of a lifetime through the Pentland Scholarship to study at NYU and UCL. Returning to higher education at forty-eight seemed a far-fetched possibility which you made happen.

I would like to thank former President Dr Ernest Bai Koroma for appointing me to serve my country as Special Gender Adviser. This appointment gave me a wonderful platform to attract many more opportunities, not only to serve my country but contribute to the global discourse on gender equality and women's empowerment.

Nothing in my life would have been possible without the loyalty of my private aides. Gina is the CEO of my life, ensuring my home is always in order. Thank you for making my home comfortable to live and work in. Your loyalty is highly appreciated. Morlai, you are my source of calm. Thank you for keeping me safe. Fatmata, you ensure my hair and nails are always properly done and thank you for your kindness in making me physically and emotionally beautiful. Sento, FA and Sembu, thank you for protecting me always. My safety as Gender Adviser to the President rested with you. I remain grateful to your high standards of professionalism.

To the army of solidarity sisters and brothers, I am humbled by your support. Special thanks to Women of Wanjama, SProWNet, the Unity Party, and the Sierra Leone Rugby Union for your contribution to my growth. To the 50th Speaker Series team, sponsors, partners and the incredible schools, thank you so much for walking the journey with me. We will continue our good work.

My daughters and sons, especially Dr Darlinda, Elizabeth – you have been outstanding, Agatha, Abdulai and Amos, thank you for the genuine love you show in your individual ways. I am grateful to have you all in my life. Because of you, I have great hopes for the next generation and the development of my country. To all my mentees, thank you for being a source of inspiration.

These incredible women and men who have consistently played the role of mother and father in my life. You ensured that I remain grounded in all I do. Your unconditional love and guidance have helped me navigate my private, professional and spiritual paths. With great love and appreciation, I say thank you to PCMP Madam Matilda Minah Lansana-Minah, PCMP Haja Fatmata Koroma-Kajue, Haja Afsatu Kabba, Aunty Aminata, Amb Dauda Kamara and Uncle Alhaji Victor Sheriff. Each one of you have made a positive impact on my life and I wouldn't be the woman I am today without your counsel.

This book would not have been published without David Horne's invitation to the Funding Circle event at the London Stock Exchange where I was fortunate to meet Lucy McCarraher of Rethink Press, my publishers. Lucy, without your understanding and empowering business approach, this book would have been an aspiration for many more years. Your guidance has led me to be an author. Thank you for your unwavering support. Sincere thanks to Verity for helping me with the book plan, and to the entire team at Rethink Press, especially Eve and Caroline for adapting to my mode of communication and for making me achieve my lifetime's dream. Special thanks to David for creating the opportunity.

Finally, all the global community of women and girls who are victims of sexual violence, especially rape, thank you for your resilience and for giving me the strength to share my story. My Special Ladies Ring of counsellors and support system: Amie Monloius, Basita Michael, Fatou Wurie, Sinkarie Robin-Coker, Margaret Kadi, Ramatu Kargbo (Precious Almond Nut), Fatmata B Jalloh, Mariam Kamara, Cecilia Greene, Delores, Isha Bestman, Aminata Kamara, Aminata Multi-Kamara, Mariama Kargbo, Mary-Ann Kaikai, Theresa Wyse, Grace Gaye and my dearest niece Sybille Monlouis – thank you! I bow to my dearest friend – the pen pusher extraordinaire – Osman Benk Sankoh for your support through my writing process. You would find all ways to get me up and writing. You have been the head boy of motivation – I appreciate your friendship, my brother – thank you!

The Author

Ms Naasu Genevieve Fofanah was born in a tiny village Foindu Perrie, Pujehun District, Sierra Leone, West Africa. She is an International Development and Public Administration professional specialising in Gender and Global Public Policy. Ms Fofanah is a Pentland Scholar and a graduate of New York University, University College London and University of Westminster.

She returned to Sierra Leone in 2009 to support the post-war development after living in the UK and US for nearly two decades. Ms Fofanah is the Founder of

Susue Consulting, Deputy Leader of the Sierra Leone Unity Party and Board Chairperson of the Sierra Leone Rugby Union. She also served as Special Gender Adviser to the erstwhile President of Sierra Leone from 2012 to 2015 and Vice Chairperson of the UNECA Bureau on Women and Development (2013–2015). Naasu is a rape survivor and has committed her life to ending rape. Proceeds from her book will go towards the construction of the Women of Wanjama women's village for victims and survivors of Rape.

Ms Fofanah lives in London and Freetown and has a daughter, JJ, who lives in New York.